GERMANY, AUSTRIA AND SWITZERLAND IN 22 DAYS

A STEP-BY-STEP GUIDE AND TRAVEL ITINERARY

BY RICK STEVES

Library of Congress Catalog No. 87-042537

Published by John Muir Publications
Santa Fe, New Mexico
Printed in U.S.A.

Design/Production   Mary Shapiro
Maps   Dave Hoerlein
Cover Map   Jennifer Dewey
Typography   Copygraphics, Inc., Santa Fe, NM

ISBN 0-912528-66-4

CONTENTS

HOW TO USE THIS BOOK

This book is the tour guide in your pocket. It lets you be the boss by giving you the best 22 days in Germany, Switzerland and Austria and a suggested way to use that time most efficiently.

Our 22 Day series is for do-it-yourselfers who would like the organization and smoothness of a tour without the straight-jacket. It's almost having your strudel and eating it too.

The "22 Days" books originated (and are still used) as hand-books for those who join me on my "Back Door Europe" tours. Since most large organized tours work to keep their masses ig-norant while visiting many of the same places we'll cover, this book is handy for anyone taking a typical big bus tour—but wanting also to maintain some independence and flexibility.

This plan is maximum thrills per mile, minute, and dollar. It's designed for travel by rental car, but is adaptable to train (see train chapter later). The pace is fast but not hectic. It's designed for the American with limited time who wants to see everything but who doesn't want the "if it's Tuesday this must be Salzburg" craziness. The plan includes the predictable "required" biggies (Rhine castles, Mozart's house and the Vienna Opera) with a good dose of "Back Door" intimacy—cozy Danube villages, thrilling mountain luge rides, Swiss chocolate factories, a Black Forest mineral spa and traffic-free Swiss Alp towns—mixed in.

Germany, Austria and Switzerland in 22 Days is balanced and streamlined, avoiding typical tourist burn-out by including only the most exciting castles and churches. I've been very selective. For example, we won't visit both the Matterhorn and the Jungfrau—just the best of the two. The "best," of course, is only my opinion. But after ten busy years of travel writing, lec-turing and tour guiding, I've developed a sixth sense of what tickles the traveler's fancy. I love this itinerary. I get excited just thinking about it.

Of course, connect-the-dots travel isn't perfect, just as color-by-numbers painting ain't good art. But this book is your friendly Franconian, your German in a jam, your handbook. It's your well-thought-out and tested itinerary. I've done it—and refined it—many times on my own and with groups (most recently in August, September and November, 1986). Use it, take advantage of it, but don't let it rule you.

Read this book before you begin your trip. Use it as a rack to hang more ideas on. As you plan, study, travel and talk to peo-ple, you'll fill this book with notes. It's your tool. The book is completely modular and is adaptable to any trip. You'll find 22 units—or days—each built with the same sections:

1. **Introductory Overview** for the day.
2. An hour-by-hour **Suggested Schedule** recommended for that day.
3. List of the most important **Sightseeing Highlights** (rated: ▲▲▲Don't miss; ▲▲Try hard to see; ▲Worthwhile if you can make it).
4. **Transportation** tips and instructions.
5. **Food** and **Accommodations**: How and where to find the best budget places, including addresses, phone numbers, and my favorites.
6. **Orientation** and easy-to-read **maps** locating all recommended places.
7. **Helpful Hints** on shopping, transportation, day-to-day chores.
8. **Itinerary options** for those with more or less than the suggested time, or with particular interests. This itinerary is *rubbery*!

My mapmaker, Dave Hoerlein, knows a good map is worth a thousand words. His maps make my text easy to follow. Dave points out all the major landmarks, streets, and accommodations mentioned in the book and he indicates the best city entry and exits for our 22 day plan. His maps are clear, concise, and readable, but are designed only to orient you and direct you until you pick up something better at the tourist information office. To get the most out of Dave's maps, learn these symbols:

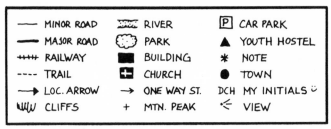

—— MINOR ROAD	▧▧ RIVER	Ⓟ CAR PARK
▬▬ MAJOR ROAD	☁ PARK	▲ YOUTH HOSTEL
++++ RAILWAY	■ BUILDING	✱ NOTE
---- TRAIL	✚ CHURCH	● TOWN
➝ LOC. ARROW	→ ONE WAY ST.	DCH MY INITIALS ‿
⋃⋃⋃ CLIFFS	+ MTN. PEAK	⩳ VIEW

At the end of the book are special chapters on post-tour options, tips on telephoning, eating and sleeping, speaking German, driving, train travel, etc.

Travel Smart
This itinerary assumes you are a well-organized traveler who
lays departure groundwork upon arrival in a town, reads a day
ahead in this book, uses the local tourist info offices, and enjoys
the hospitality of the Germanic people. Ask questions. Most
locals are eager to point you in their idea of the right direction.
Use the telephone, wear a moneybelt, use a small pocket
notebook to organize your thoughts and make simplicity a vir-
tue. If you insist on being confused, your trip will be a mess.
Those who expect to travel smart, do.

Cost
This trip's cost breaks down like this: A basic round trip USA—
Frankfurt flight—$400-800 (depending on the season and
where you fly from). A three-week car rental (split between two
people, including tax, insurance, and gas) or three weeks of rail
and bus travel—$350. For room and board figure $30 a day,
double occupancy—$660. This is more than feasible, and if
necessary, you can travel cheaper (see *Europe Through the
Back Door* for the skills and tricks of budget travel). Add $200
or $300 fun money and you've got yourself a great European
adventure for under $2,000.

When to Go
July and August are peak season—best weather and the busiest
schedule of tourist fun, but very crowded, most difficult, and
more expensive. Most of us travel during this period, so this
book tackles peak season problems, especially that of finding a
room. Early arrivals, calling ahead, and utilizing local information sources are some of the remedies I'll discuss.
    "Shoulder season" travel (May, early June, September, and
early October) is ideal. Try to plan a shoulder season trip for:
minimal crowds, decent weather, sights and tourist fun spots
still open, and the joy of being able to just grab a room almost
whenever and wherever you like.
    Winter travelers find absolutely no crowds but many sights
and accommodations are closed or run on a limited schedule.
The weather can be cold and dreary and nighttime will draw
the shades on your sightseeing well before dinner time. The
weather is predictably unpredictable but you may find the
climate chart in the back of this book helpful.

Prices & Times
    I've priced things in local currencies throughout the book.
Figure about 2 Deutsch Marks (DM) per dollar, 15 Austrian
Shillings (AS) per dollar, and 1.6 Swiss Francs per dollar.

To convert prices to dollars in your head, keep it simple: Divide DM in half, cut SF prices by a third, and cut AS a third and divide by 10. So: 36 DM = $18, 75 SF = $50, and 800 AS = about $50.

I haven't cluttered this book with many minor prices (e.g. specific admission fees and student discounts etc.). Small charges of less than a dollar shouldn't affect your sightseeing decisions.

Prices as well as hours, telephone numbers, and so on are accurate as of August, 1986. Things are always changing and I've tossed timidity out the window knowing you'll understand that this book, like any guidebook, starts to yellow before it's even printed. These countries are more stable than most European countries, but do what you can to double-check hours and times when you arrive.

This book is best consumed before 1989. If this book is no longer fresh for your tour (there will be a more recent edition), it is the prices, details about accommodations, along with some times and phone numbers that will have to be discounted. Basic sightseeing ideas should be good well into the next millennium— barring unforeseen military or volcanic activity.

I have used the 24 hour clock (or "military" time) throughout this book. After noon, instead of pm times, you'll see 13:00, 14:00 and so on. (Just add the "normal" pm hour to 12). Sooner or later you'll need to get comfortable with this standard European time system.

The hours listed are for peak season. Many places close an hour earlier in off season. Some are open only on weekends or are closed entirely in the winter. Confirm your sightseeing plans locally—especially when traveling between October and May.

Borders, Passports, Visas and Shots

Traveling throughout this region requires only a passport. No shots, and no visas. Border crossings between Germany, Switzerland and Austria are extremely easy. Sometimes you won't even have to stop—just wave your passport at the guards as you roll through. When you change countries, however, you do change money, postage stamps, and much more.

You'll be dealing with great cultural diversity. Work to adapt. The USA is huge, but it's bound by a common nationality. The cultural stew of Europe is wonderfully complex. We just assume Germany is 'Germany'; but Germany is 'Tedesco' to the Italians, 'Allemagne' to the French, and 'Deutschland' to the people who live there. While we think shower curtains are logical, many countries just cover the toilet paper and let the rest of the room shower with you. Europeans give their 'ones' an upswing and cross their 'sevens.' If you don't adapt, your 'seven' will be mistaken for a sloppy 'one' and you'll miss your train.

Keeping Up with the News (If you must)
To keep in touch with world and American news while traveling in Europe, I use the *International Herald Tribune* which comes out almost daily via satellite from many places in Europe. Every Tuesday the European editions of *Time* and *Newsweek* hit the stands. They are full of articles of particular interest to European travelers. Remember, news in English will only be sold where there's enough demand—in big cities and tourist centers. If you are concerned about how some event might affect your safety as an American traveling abroad, call the U.S. consulate or embassy in the nearest big city for advice. The best way to keep in touch with loved ones back home is to periodically call home direct. Most phone booths and hotels are set up for this. (See "Telephoning" in back.)

Terrorism
Terrorism has no business affecting your travel plans. I spent ("survived") the summer of '86 in Europe. The general feeling there among locals and travelers was 1) Reagan decided to keep America home this year to boost our economy, and 2) our media loves a crisis—and if there isn't one handy, they'll create it. I felt no unusual anti-American sentiment and I traveled knowing that, regardless of what Ronald Reagan, Dan Rather and my grandma say, you're safer (and happier) traveling in Europe.

Ugly Americanism
We travel all the way to Europe to experience something different—to become temporary locals. Americans have a knack for finding certain truths to be God-given and self-evident—things like cold beer, a bottomless coffee cup, long hot showers, and bigger being better. One of the beauties of travel is the opportunity to see that there are logical, civil, and even better alternatives.

If there is a European image of you and me, we are big, loud, a bit naive, aggressive, and rich. Still, I find warmth and friendliness throughout the Continent. An eagerness to go local and an ability—when something's not to my liking—to change my liking, makes sure I enjoy a full dose of this European hospitality. Fit in. If the bed's too short, the real problem is you're too long.

Scheduling

Your overall itinerary is a fun challenge. Read through this book and note special days (festivals, colorful market days, closed days for sights etc.). Sundays have pros and cons as they do for travelers in the USA (special events, limited hours, shops and banks closed, limited public transportation, no rush hours). Saturdays are virtually weekdays. Popular places are even more popular on weekends. Most sights are closed during one week day.

It's good to alternate intense and relaxed periods. Every trip (and every traveler) needs at least a few slack days. I followed the Biblical "one in seven" idea . . . religiously. . .on my last trip. Stretching this trip to 28 or 30 days would be much more comfortable.

To give you a little rootedness, I've minimized one night stands. Two nights in a row, even with a hectic travel day before and after, is less grueling than changing accommodations daily.

The daily suggested schedules and optional plans take many many factors into account. I don't explain most of these but I hope you take the schedules seriously.

Car Rental

If you plan to drive, rent a car through your travel agent well before departure. Car rental for this tour is much cheaper when arranged in the USA rather than in Germany. You'll want a weekly rate with unlimited mileage. Plan to pick up the car at the Frankfurt Airport and drop it off there at the end of your trip. Remember, if you drop it early or keep it longer, you'll be credited or charged at a fair, pro-rated price. Every major car rental agency has a Frankfurt Airport office. Comparison-shop through your agent.

I normally rent the smallest, least-expensive model (e.g., Ford Fiesta). For a bigger, more roomy and powerful inexpensive car, move up to the Ford 1.3-liter Escort or VW Polo category. For peace of mind, I splurge for the CDW (collision damage waiver) insurance which gives a zero-deductible rather than the standard $1,000-deductible. Remember, mini-buses are a great budget way to go for 5 to 9 people.

Car vs. Eurail

While this tour is designed for car travel, a chapter in the back of the book adapts it for train travel. With a few exceptions, trains cover this entire itinerary wonderfully. A three week first class Eurailpass costs $350 and is best for single travelers, those who'll be spending more time in big cities and those who don't want to drive in Europe. While a car gives you the ultimate in mobility and freedom, enables you to search for hotels more

easily and carries your bags for you, the train zips you effortlessly from city to city dropping you normally in the center and
near the tourist office. Cars are great in the countryside but a
worthless headache in places like Munich, Bern and Vienna. To
go by car or train . . . that is the question. And for this itinerary,
I'd drive.

Recommended Guidebooks

This small book is only your itinerary handbook. To really enjoy and appreciate these busy three weeks, you'll also need a
directory-type guidebook and some good maps. I know it hurts
to spend $30 or $40 on extra books and maps, but when you
consider the improvements they'll make in your $2,000
vacation—not to mention the money they'll save you—not
buying them would be perfectly "penny-wise and pound
foolish." Here's my recommended list of supplemental information needed:

To Consider Buying Before You Leave

1. A general low-budget directory-type guidebook—that
is, a fatter book than this one, listing a broader range of accommodations, restaurants, sights, etc. Which one you choose
depends on your budget and style of travel. My favorite by far is
Let's Go: Europe, written and thoroughly updated every year
by Harvard students (new editions come out around January).
Let's Go covers big cities, villages, the countryside, art, entertainment, budget room and board, transportation, etc. It's written for students on a student's budget and even though I'm
neither, I use it every year. If its youthful approach isn't yours,
and you've got plenty of money, then try Arthur Frommer's
Dollarwise guides to Germany, Switzerland and Austria.
2. A cultural and sightseeing guide—The tall green Michelin
guides (Germany, Austria, and Switzerland) have nothing about
room and board but everything else you'll ever need to know
about the sights, customs and culture. They are excellent
(especially for drivers) and available in Europe. A small German
phrasebook and dictionary is also helpful.
3. Europe Through the Back Door (by Rick Steves) gives
you the basic skills, the foundations which make this demanding 22-day plan possible. Chapters on: minimizing jet lag,
packing light, driving vs. train travel, finding budget beds
without reservations, changing money, theft, travel
photography, long distance telephoning in Europe, ugly-
Americanism, traveler's toilet trauma, laundry, and itinerary
strategies and techniques. The book also includes special articles on 38 exciting nooks and undiscovered European cran-
nies which I call "Back Doors."

4. Europe 101: History and Art for Travelers (by Rick
Steves and Gene Openshaw) tells you the story of these cultures
in a practical, fun to read 360-page package. Ideal for those who
want to be able to step into a Gothic cathedral and excitedly
nudge their partner saying "Isn't this a marvelous improvement
over Romanesque!"

Books and Maps to Buy in Europe
Maps—Most bookstores, especially in touristed areas, have a
good selection of maps. For this tour I picked up the
Bundesrepublik Deutschland Auto Atlas (by RV Reise und
Verkehrsverlag, 1:200,000 scale) for Germany and the Osterreich Strassen Atlas (also by RV R. und V., 1:300,000 scale)
for Austria. Each of these atlases has a good coverage of the entire country with an extensive index and handy maps of all
major cities. For Switzerland I got by with Michelin maps #216
and 217 (or Die General Karte maps #1 and 2) with 1:200,000
scale. Throughout the tour you'll be picking up free maps of
cities and regions at local tourist offices.

Freedom
This book's goal is to free you, not chain you. Please defend
your spontaneity like you would your mother. Use this book to
sort this region's myriad sights into the most interesting,
representative, diverse, and efficient 22 days of travel. Use it
to avoid time- and money-wasting mistakes, to get more intimate with Europe by traveling without a tour—as a temporary
local person. And use it as a point of departure from which
to shape *your* best possible travel experience. Only a real
dullard would follow this entire plan exactly as I've laid it out.
     Anyone who has read this far has what it takes intellectually
to do this tour on their own. Be confident, militantly positive, relish the challenge and rewards of doing your own planning.

Send Me a Postcard, Drop Me a Line. . .
While I do what I can to keep this book accurate and up-to-
date, things are always changing. If you enjoy a successful trip
with the help of this book and would like to share your discov-
eries (and make my job a lot easier), please send in any tips,
recommendations, criticisms or corrections to 120 4th N.,
Edmonds, WA 98020. All correspondents will receive a year's
subscription to our "Back Door Travel" quarterly newsletter
(it's free anyway. . .), and recommendations used will get you
a free copy of my next edition.
     Thanks, and "Gute Reise!"

BACK DOOR PHILOSOPHY

AS TAUGHT IN EUROPE THROUGH THE BACK DOOR

TRAVEL IS INTENSIFIED LIVING—maximum thrills per minute and one of the last great sources of legal adventure. In many ways, the less you spend the more you get.

Experiencing the real thing requires candid informality— going "Through the Back Door."

Traditional travel writing give its readers an eloquent void—a thousand column inches wide. Rick Steves' books will fill that hole, preparing and encouraging you to experience the world—from Walla Walla to Bora Bora.

We'll discuss problems and offer solutions, bolstered by cocky optimism. Too much travel writing comes from free trips. A guest of a country's tourist industry gains experience helpful only to other guests of the industry. We travel the way you will, making mistakes so you can learn from them. We'll dispel myths and conquer fears and apprehensions that inhibit travelers. We'll widen your comfort zone. Here are a few beliefs:

Affording travel is a matter of priorities. Many people who "can't afford a trip" could sell their car and travel for two years.

You can travel anywhere in the world for $25 a day plus transportation costs. Money has little to do with enjoying your trip. In fact, in many ways, the less you spend the more you get—spending more money only builds a thicker wall between you and what you came to see.

A tight budget forces you to travel "close to the ground," meeting and communicating with the people, not relying on service with a purchased smile. Never sacrifice sleep, nutrition, safety or cleanliness in the name of budget. Simply enjoy the local-style alternatives to expensive hotels and restaurants.

Americans are generally too things-oriented to travel well. Travel like Gandhi—with simple clothes, open eyes and an uncluttered mind. 'Tis a gift to be simple. If things aren't to your liking, don't change the things—change your liking.

Extroverts have more fun. If your trip is low on magic moments, kick yourself and start making things happen. Dignity and good travel don't mix. Leave your beeper at home and let your hair down.

If you don't enjoy a place it's often because you don't know enough about it. Seek out the truth. Recognize tourist traps.

A culture is legitimized by its existence. Give a people the benefit of your open mind. Think of things as different but not better or worse.

Of course, travel, like the world, is a series of hills and valleys. Be fanatically positive and militantly optimistic.

Travel is addicting. It can make you a happier American, as well as a citizen of the world. Our Earth is home to five billion equally important people. That's wonderfully humbling.

Globetrotting destroys ethnocentricity and encourages the understanding and appreciation of various cultures. Travel changes people. Many travelers toss aside their "hometown blinders," assimiliating the best points of different cultures into their own character.

The world is a cultural garden. We're working on the ultimate salad. Won't you join us?

GERMANY, AUSTRIA AND SWITZERLAND

DAY 1   You'll fly into Frankfurt, the most direct and least expensive German destination from the USA. Pick up your rental car and drive to the famous medieval fairytale town of Rothenburg for your first night.

DAY 2   Spend all of today exploring Germany's best-preserved walled town. Walk the wall, visit the exquisite carved altar and the fascinating medieval crime and punishment museum, and enjoy Germany's best shopping town.

DAY 3   Today we drive south, exploring the "Romantic Road" through the picturesque villages, farmhouses and onion-domed churches deep into the medieval heartland of Bavaria, and finally crossing into Austria. After hiking up to the Ehrenburg ruined castle and screaming down a nearby skislope in a special summer-only wheeled luge on a concrete slalom course we'll catch our breath for the evening in the Tyrolean town of Reutte, Austria.

DAY 4—This is Castle Day and nearby, back in Germany, is "Mad Ludwig's" Disney-type Neuschwanstein castle. After touring Europe's most spectacular castle, stop by the Wies church—a textbook example of Bavarian Rococo bursting with curly curlicues, and visit Germany's wood-carving capital, Oberammergau, to window shop and tour the great Passion Play Theater. Fill the afternoon with more of King Ludwig's extravagances, this time in his more liveable Linderhof palace. Back in Reutte, slap dance and yodel with a Tyrolean Folk Evening.

DAY 5   Dilly-dally through three hours of Bavarian beauty north to Munich. Spend the afternoon orienting yourself in the old center of town with its colorful pedestrian mall. Evenings are best spent in Munich's crazy beerhalls— great oom-pah music, rowdy Bavarian atmosphere, big beers, big pretzels, and no-nonsense buxom beer maids who pull mustard packets from their cleavages.

DAY 6   Today is spent immersed in Munich's art and history—crown jewels, Baroque theater, Wittelsbach palaces, great art, beautiful parks and gardens.

DAY 7   And on the seventh day we'll rest—but only until noon when we autobahn south to Salzburg, visiting Hitler's mountain hideaway, Berchtesgaden, on the way. We'll tour a fun

Germany, Switzerland & Austria in 22 Days

salt mine putting on an old miner's outfit, riding the tiny train into the mountain to slide down long splinter-free bannisters, cruise subterranean lakes and learn about old-fashioned salt mining.

DAY 8   After enjoying the sights and castle of Salzburg, leave Mozart's hometown for Sound of Music country. After a very scenic afternoon in the Salzkammergut Lake District (alive with the S.O.M.) check into a private home in the postcard-pretty fjord-cuddling town of Hallstatt.

DAY 9   Take a short intermission from Austria's fairytales to make a pilgrimage to the powerful Mauthausen concentration camp. Then follow the Danube through its most romantic section, lined with ruined castles, glorious abbeys, vineyards upon vineyard, small towns, and on into Vienna.

DAY 10   Vienna, the easternmost tip and most exciting historic and cultural city of this tour, was the Hapsburg capital. It excels in art, tombs, palaces, pastries, coffee shops, and music. In other words, you'll be very busy today.

DAY 11   After another Vienna morning and the afternoon at the Schonbrunn Palace, Versailles' eastern rival, autobahn five hours west to Innsbruck, sleeping in a nearby village.

DAY 12 After some Alpine joy-riding you'll cross into Switzerland. Appenzell—traditional and cozy—is the best first taste of Heidi Land. This is cowbell country, no staggering mountains yet, just a chance to savor the small-town ambience of a country whose cities have become quite sleek and modern.

DAY 13 Today we visit the Ballenberg Open Air Folk Museum. Countless historic buildings have been moved to this huge park to give us tourists an intimate walk through every corner of Switzerland's diverse culture. Thirty minutes away is the grand old resort of Interlaken, and south of there, a gondola will lift you high above the valley into the terrific traffic-free Alpine village of Gimmelwald.

DAY 14 Today we'll learn why they say "If Heaven isn't what it's cracked up to be send me back to Gimmelwald." All day is free to frolic and hike, high above the stress and clouds of the real world. This is your vacation from your busy vacation. Recharge your touristic batteries.

DAY 15 After a morning hike, drive south to Lake Geneva to tour the very romantic Chateau Chillon and enjoy a taste of French-speaking Switzerland.

DAY 16 For the highlights of French Switzerland, we'll tour the resort towns and rugged wine road of Lake Geneva, the spectacularly set hometown of Gruyere cheese, and a nearby chocolate factory. We'll spend the evening in Murten—Switzerland's best preserved walled town.

DAY 17 Today is for the Swiss capital—Bern. Stately but human, classy but fun, Bern is the best look at urban Switzerland. For dinner, drive into Germany's Black Forest to the charming and overlooked village of Staufen.

DAY 18 The Black Forest is filled with tourists and cuckoo clocks. It's also swimming with soothing mineral spas, Germany's healthiest air and sunniest climate, traditional villages and folk fests and wonderful wooded drives. After a quick look at the city of Freiburg, we'll enjoy a scenic drive through the heart of this legendary forest, and find our hotel in Baden Baden. Today's grand finale, a two hour "Roman Irish" bath complete with massage, will show you why this place was Europe's leading spa a hundred years ago.

DAY 19   Today we drive to Roman Trier, Germany's oldest city, and explore the peaceful Mosel River from there to the pleasant village of Zell.

DAY 20   Explore more of the sleepy Mosel, so much more relaxing than the busy and industrial Rhine. After touring Germany's most exciting medieval castle, Berg Eltz, we'll drive to Bonn.

DAY 21   Today we break again from storybook Germany to sample two real no-nonsense cities. Bonn is West Germany's capital and a colorful modern university city. Koln, which, like most German cities, rose gleaming and muscular from the ashes of WWII, is a cheery modern city with Germany's finest Gothic cathedral and some excellent art.

DAY 22   Our grand finale is a day of cruising the Rhine and climbing through its castles. We'll cruise from Koblenz to Mainz and tour Rheinfels castle above the town of St. Goar.

When you return to Frankfurt the circle is complete and you've experienced the best 22 days Germany, Switzerland, and Austria have to offer. Of course, next year you may want 22 more.

DAY 1

DEPART USA—FRANKFURT

Call before going to the airport to confirm departure time as scheduled. Expect delays. Bring something to do—a book, a journal, some handwork—to make any waits easy on yourself. Remember, no matter how long it takes, flying to Europe is a very easy way to get there.

To minimize jet lag (body clock adjustment, stress):
■ Leave well rested. Pretend you're leaving a day earlier than you really are. Plan accordingly and enjoy a peaceful last day at home.
■ During the flight minimize stress by eating lightly, avoiding alcohol, caffeine, and sugar. Drink juice.
■ Sleep through the in-flight movie—or at least close your eyes and fake it.

GERMANY

95,000 square miles (smaller than Oregon).
62 million people (more than Oregon, about 650 per square mile, and declining slowly).
One Deutsch Mark = 50 cents, 2 DM = $1.

Ja, Deutschland. Energetic, efficient, organized, and Europe's economic muscleman. 85% of its people live in cities and average earnings are among the highest on earth. 97% of the workers get a one-month paid vacation, and during the other eleven months they create a gross national product of about one-third the USA's. Germany has risen from the ashes of WWII to become the world's fifth biggest industrial power, ranking fourth in steel output and nuclear power, third in automobile production. It shines culturally, beating out all but two countries in production of books, Nobel laureates and professors. And its bustling new cities are designed to make people feel happy to be there.

While northern Germany is Protestant and the populace assaults life aggressively, southern Germany is Catholic, more relaxed and leisurely. The southern German, or Bavarian, dialect is to High (northern) German what the dialect of Alabama or Georgia is to the northern USA. This historic north-south division is less pronounced these days as Germany becomes a more and more mobile society.

Germany's most interesting tourist route today—Rhine,
Romantic Road, Bavaria—was yesterday's most important trade
route, where Germany's most prosperous and important
medieval cities were located. Remember, Germany as a nation is
just barely 100 years old. In 1850 there were 35 independent
countries in what is now Germany. In medieval times there
were over 300, each with its own weights, measures, coinage
and king. Many were surrounded by what we would call iron
curtains. This helps explain the many diverse customs found in
such a compact land. The American image of Germany is
Bavaria (probably because that was "our" sector immediately
after the war) where the countryside is most traditional.

Practice your German energetically because all but two days
of this tour are in German-speaking country. For bitter or
wurst, you'll have to learn a little Deutsch.

Germans eat lunch from 12 noon to 3 pm and dinner between 6 pm and 9 pm. Each region has its own gastronomic
twist, so order local house specials whenever possible. Fish and
venison are good and don't miss the sauerkraut. Great beer and
white wines abound. Try the small local brands. "Gummi Bears"
are a local gumdrop candy with a cult following (beware of
imitations—you must see the word "Gummi"), and Nutella is
a chocolate nut spread specialty that may change your life.

Banks are generally open 8 am-12:30 pm and 1:30 pm-4 pm,
other offices from 8 am to 4 pm. August is a holiday month for
workers—but that doesn't really affect us tourists.

ARRIVE IN FRANKFURT!

How much you do today depends on what time your flight
arrives. It's best to plan an easy first day or two in Europe. Today
will be a smashing success if you arrive safely, travel to Rothenburg (pron. ROW-ten-burg) and get settled. Since most flights
will get you in by midday, we'll figure on a couple hours of
sightseeing along Germany's Romantic Road before reaching
Rothenburg.

Suggested Schedule	
?	Arrive at Frankfurt airport. Pick up reserved car, hit the autobahn. If early, visit Wurzburg. Take Romantic Road from Bad Mergentheim to Rothenburg.
17:00	Check into Rothenburg hotel. Quiet evening.
Sleep	Rothenburg.

When flying to Europe, you always lose a day; if you leave on a Tuesday, you'll land on Wednesday. Frankfurt's airport (Flughaven), just a 12-minute train ride from downtown (6 trips/hour, 3DM or $1.50), is very efficient and "user friendly." It has everything an airport could need—showers ($3), baggage check ($1/day), banks open 7:30-21:00 with fair rates, a handy train station, a decent waiting lounge where you can sleep overnight, easy rental car pick-up, plenty of parking, and an information booth.

The most important chores upon arrival in Frankfurt are to call your Rothenburg hotel to reserve or reconfirm your room, change a couple of hundred dollars into Deutsch Marks, and leave. If you're driving, pick up your car and follow the green autobahn signs for Wurzburg.

Train travelers can validate their Eurailpass or buy a ticket at the airport station where they'll catch a train directly to Wurzburg and connect to Rothenburg.

Sightseeing Highlights between Frankfurt and Rothenburg

▲▲ **Wurzburg**—A historic city, though freshly rebuilt since WWII, Wurzburg is worth a stop to see its impressive Prince Bishop's Residenz and its bubbly Baroque chapel (Hofkirche). This is a Franconian Versailles with grand stairways, 3-D art, and a huge fresco by Tiepolo. Tag along with a tour if you can find one in English or buy the fine little $1 guidebook. Be sure to check out the sculptured gardens. Open daily 9:00-17:00 April-September (closed Mondays), and 10:00-15:30 October-March. Last entry one-half hour before closing, admission 3.50 DM. Easy parking, short walk from station.

▲▲▲ **Romantic Road (Romantische Strasse)**—The best way to connect Frankfurt and Munich or Fussen is via the popular Romantic Road. This path winds you past the most beautiful towns and scenery of Germany's medieval heartland. Any tourist office can give you a brochure listing the many interesting Baroque palaces, lovely carved altarpieces, and walled medieval cities you'll pass along the way.

From Wiesbaden, Frankfurt or Wurzburg in the north, to Munich or Fussen in the south, the route includes these highlights:

Wurzburg—Old town along Main River under Marienburg fortress. Outstanding Baroque Prince Bishop's Residenz and chapel.

Weikersheim—Palace with fine Baroque gardens (prime picnic spot), folk museum and fine old square.

Herrgottskapelle—One mile from Creglingen, Tilman Riemenschneider's greatest carved altarpiece in a peaceful church. Fast and fun "finger hut" (thimble) museum just across the street. Both sights open till 18:00 and only 1 DM.

Rothenburg o.d. Tauber—See tomorrow's plan.

Dinkelsbuhl—Rothenburg's little sister, cute, beautifully preserved walled town. Twenty towers and gates surround this picturesque town. "Kinderzeche" children's festival turns this town wonderfully on end each mid-July. Tourist info tel. 09851-3031.

Rottenbuch—Impressive church, nondescript village in lovely setting.

Wieskirche—The best Baroque-Rococo church in Germany. In a sweet meadow. Outstanding!

Newschwanstein—Mad King Ludwig's Disney-esque castle, described later.

The drive in general gives you a good look at rural Germany. My favorite sections are from Weikersheim to Rothenburg and from Landsberg to Fussen. By car, simply follow the green "Romantische Strasse" signs.

By train . . . take the bus. The Europa Bus Company makes this trip twice a day in each direction. The ride costs about $40 but is free with a Eurailpass. Each bus has a guide who hands out brochures and narrates the journey in English, with stops for about an hour in the towns of Rothenburg and Dinkelsbuhl and quickly at a few other attractions. There is no quicker or easier way to travel across Germany and get such a good dose of the countryside.

Bus reservations aren't necessary (except possibly on a summer weekend, call 069/7903240 three days in advance) and you can stop over where you like. Refer to the timetable at the end of this book.

Frankfurt—Probably a nice place to live, but I wouldn't want to visit there. Don't visit Frankfurt unless your only alternative is killing time at the airport before flying home. If that happens, pick up a city map at the tourist information office (T.I.) in the station, walk down sleazy Kaiserstrasse past Goethe's house (a very mediocre sight) to Romerberg, Frankfurt's lively market square. A string of museums is just across the river along Schaumainkai (all open Tues-Sat, 10:00-17:00). Whatever you do, don't drive or sleep in Frankfurt.

Transportation

The 2 ½ hour drive from the airport to Rothenburg is something even a jet-lagged zombie can handle. The airport is right on the Wurzburg freeway. It's a 90 minute, 75-mile straight shot to Wurzburg. The "Spessart" reststop about half-way there has a tourist info office with a friendly man who can telephone Rothenburg—and speak German for you.

Take the "Wurzburg/Stuttgart/Ulm road 19" exit and follow #19 south to Bad Mergenheim where a very scenic slice of the Romantic Road will lead you right into Rothenburg. If you're plugging in a stop at Wurzburg, take the later "Heidingsfeld-Wurzburg" exit and follow the signs to "Stadmitte," then to "Residenz." To leave Wurzburg, follow the Stuttgart/Ulm road 19 signs from the center of town south.

Train travelers will have missed the Romantic Road bus on this first day of arrival so will have to go straight to Rothenburg with a possible stop in Wurzburg. (The Residenz is just a short walk from the station). The train ride from the airport to Rothenburg goes airport—Frankfurt Central—Wurzburg—Steinach—Rothenburg with trains departing from the airport at 7:00, 9:00, 10:00, 11:00, 13:00, 15:00 and 16:00, from Frankfurt Central 21 minutes later, arriving in Wurzburg in about 2 hours and arriving in Rothenburg (after a change in Steinach) in approximately 3½ hours. The Romantic Road bus tour leaves from Europa bus stops next to the Frankfurt station (south side, 8:15 departure daily) and at the Wurzburg station (daily 9:00, never full).

Food and Lodging

Rothenburg is crowded with visitors (including what is probably Europe's greatest single concentration of Japanese tourists), but finding a room is no problem. From the main square (which has a tourist office with room-finding service), just walk downhill on Schmiedgasse street until it becomes Spitalgasse. This street has plenty of gasthauses, zimmers ($10 per person with breakfast) and two fine $3-a-night youth hostels (in German, "Jugendherberge," tel. 09861-4510).

I stay in Spitalgasse #28 **Hotel Goldene Rose**, tel. 09861-4638, for about $12 a night. Less expensive yet and very friendly is a room in the home of **Herr Moser** on Spitalgasse #12 (tel. 5971). Also good is **Gastehaus Raidel** (Wenggasse #3, tel. 3115, 24 DM per person, will hold a room for a phone call), **Pension Poschel** (Wenggasse 22, tel. 3430, 20 DM), **Pension Becker** (Rosengasse 23, tel 5562, 22 DM) and the friendly zimmer of English-speaking **George and Frida Ohr** (Untere Schmiedgasse #6 near the criminal museum, tel. 4966, 40 DM doubles).

For a peaceful night in a nearby village consider the clean, quiet, and comfortable old **Gasthof Zum Schwarzen Lamm** in the town of Detwang just below Rothenburg (50 DM doubles). While they serve good food, the Eulestube is a local style restaurant nearby full of happy campers. For more village zimmers look in Detwang or in little Bettwar a bit further down the road.

DAY 2
ROTHENBURG OB DER TAUBER

Today we stay put, getting over jet lag and enjoying Europe's most exciting medieval town. Rothenburg is well worth two nights and a whole day. In the Middle Ages, when Frankfurt and Munich were just wide spots in the road, Rothenburg was Germany's second largest city with a whopping population of 6,000. Today it's her best-preserved medieval walled town, enjoying tremendous tourist popularity without losing its charm.

Suggested Schedule	
7:00	Walk on wall.
8:30	Breakfast.
9:00	T.I. to confirm plans, walking tour? Climb tower, visit St. Jacob's Church, tour Criminal Museum, buy picnic.
12:00	Picnic in castle garden, rest.
14:00	Shopping or walk through the countryside.
Sleep	Rothenburg.

Too often Rothenburg brings out the shopper in visitors before they've had a chance to appreciate the historic city. True, this is a great place to do your German shopping, but first see the town. The T.I. on the market square has guided tours in English. If none are scheduled, hire a private guide. For about $25, a local historian—who's usually an intriguing character as well—will bring the ramparts alive. A thousand years of history are packed between the cobbles. Call Karen Bierstedt, tel. 09861-2217, or Manfred Baumann, tel. 4146.

First, pick up a map and information at the T.I. on the main square (open 9:00-18:00, on Sat 9:00-12:00, closed Sun). Confirm sightseeing plans and ask about the daily 13:30 walking tour and evening entertainment (tel. 40492).

To orient yourself, think of the town map as a human head. Its nose (the castle) sticks out to the left, the neck is the lower panhandle part (with the youth hostels and my favorite hotel).

Sightseeing Highlights
▲ **Walk the Wall**—1½ miles around, great views, good orientation. Can be done speedily in one hour, requires no special sense of balance. Photographers will go through lots of film. Ideal before breakfast or at sunset.

▲▲ **Climb Town Hall Tower**—Best view of town and sur-rounding countryside. Open 9:30-12:30, 13:00-17:00, 1 DM. Rigorous but interesting climb.

▲▲ **Medieval Crime and Punishment Museum**—The best of its kind, full of fascinating old legal bits and pieces, instru-ments of punishment and torture, even a special cage—com-plete with a metal gag—for nags. Exhibits in English. Open 9:30-19:00, 4 DM.

▲▲ **St. Jacob's Church**—Here you'll find a glorious 500-year-old Riemenschneider altarpiece located up the stairs and behind the organ. Riemenschneider was the Michelangelo of German woodcarvers. This is the one "must see" art treasure in town. Open daily 9:30-17:30, Sun 10:30-17:30, 2 DM.

Meistertrunk Show, Main Square at 11:00, 12:00, 13:00, 14:00, 15:00, 21:00, or 22:00—For the ritual gathering of the tourists to see the breathtaking reenactment of the Meistertrunk story. You'll learn about the town's most popular legend, a fun, if fan-ciful, story. Hint: for the best show, don't watch the clock, watch the open-mouthed tourists.

▲ **Walk in the Countryside**—Just below the Burggarten (castle garden) in the Tauber Valley is the cute, skinny 600-year-old castle/summer home of Mayor Toppler (open 10:00-12:00 and 14:00-17:00). It's furnished intimately and is well worth a look. Notice the photo of bombed out 1945 Rothenburg on the top floor. Across from the castle a radiantly happy lady will show you her 800-year-old water-powered flour mill called the Fuchsmuhle. From here you can walk on past the covered bridge and huge trout to the peaceful village of Detwang. Detwang is actually older than Rothenburg, with another great Riemen-schneider altarpiece.

Swimming—Rothenburg has a great modern recreation center with an outdoor pool, a few minutes walk down the Dinkelsbuhl Road, open 10:00-20:00, 2 DM.

Franconian Open Air Museum—Twenty minutes drive from Rothenburg in the undiscovered "Rothenburgy" town of Bad Windsheim is a small open air folk museum that, compared with others in Europe, isn't much, but is trying very hard and gives you the best look around at traditional rural Franconia.

Shopping
Rothenburg is one of Germany's best shopping towns. Make a point to do your shopping here. Lovely prints, carvings, wine glasses, Christmas tree ornaments and beer steins are very popular. The "Friese" shop (just west of the tourist office on the corner across from the public w.c.) is friendly, good and gives shoppers with this book tremendous service: a 10% discount, 14% tax deducted if you have it mailed, postage at cost, and

a free Rothenburg map. Anneliese who runs the place with her
kids, Jurgen and Berni, even changes money at the best rates in
town with no extra charge. Hummel figurines, apparently, are
sold at regulated prices throughout Germany.

For those who prefer to eat their souvenirs, the Backereis,
with their succulent pastries, pies and cakes, are pleasantly
distracting. Skip the good looking but bad tasting "Rothen-
burger Schnee Balls."

Evening Fun and Beer Drinking
The best beer garden for summer evenings is just outside the
wall at the Rodertor. Closer to home, enjoy good wine, fun
accordian music and a surly waiter (21:00 except Tues and Sun)
at Plonlein #4.

Itinerary Options
This "two nights and a full day" plan assumes you have a car.
Eurailers taking the Romantic Road bus tour must leave around
13:30 so you'll have to decide between half a day or 1½ days
here. For sightseeing, half a day is enough. For a rest after jet
lag, a day and a half sounds better.

A popular pastime seems to be the search for "little, untouristy Rothenburgs." There are many (Michelstadt, Miltenberg, Bamberg, Bad Windsheim, Dinkelsbuhl, and others I decided to forget) but none holds a candle to the king of medieval German cuteness. Rothenburg is best even with crowds and over-priced souvenirs. Save time and mileage and be satisfied with the winner.

DAY 3

ROMANTIC ROAD TO TYROL

Today we wind through Bavaria's Romantic Road, stopping wherever the cows look friendly or a village fountain beckons. After a glimpse of Europe's most fairy-tale castle, we'll cross into Tyrolia in Austria to explore the desolate ruins of a Medieval castle and finish the day with an evening of slap dancing, yodelling and local music.

Suggested Schedule	
7:30	Breakfast.
8:30	Romantic Road, head for Austria.
9:30	Stop in Dinkelsbuhl, buy picnic.
10:00	Drive south on Romantic Road, picnicking en route to Austrian border.
14:00	Cross into Austria, check into Reutte hotel.
15:00	Hike to Ehrenburg ruins.
16:30	Luge ride down ski slope in a go-cart.
18:00	Rest and dinner.
20:30	Tyrolean folk evening.

Get an early start to enjoy the quaint hills and rolling villages of what was long ago Germany's major medieval trade route. After a quick stop in Dinkelsbuhl, cross the baby Danube River (Donau in German) and continue south along the Romantic Road to Fussen. Drive by Neuschwanstein castle just to sweeten your dreams before crossing into Austria to get set up at Reutte.

Reutte (pronounced ROY-teh, rolled r), population 5,000, is a relaxed town, popular with Germans and Austrians for its climate (doctors recommend its "grade 1" air), yet it's far from the international tourist crowd.

If the weather's good, we'll hike to the mysterious castle ruins and ride the luge. Finish your day off with a slap-dancing bang at a Tyrolean folk evening.

Sightseeing Highlights
▲ **Dinkelsbuhl**—Just a small Rothenburg without the mobs, but cute enough to merit a short stop. Park near the church in the center, buy a picnic and just browse. You'll find an interesting local museum, a well-preserved medieval wall, towers, gates, and a moat.
▲▲ **Ehrenburg Ruins**— The ruined castle of Ehrenburg broods over Reutte, capping a nearby hilltop. From the car park, it's a steep 20-minute hike for a great view from your own

private ruined castle. For more castle mystique climb 30 minutes more up the larger neighboring hill to a bigger, more desolate, overgrown, and romantic ruin and imagine how proud Count Meinrad II of Tyrol (who built the castle in 1290) would be to know that his castle repelled 16,000 Swedish soldiers in 1632.

▲▲ **Sommerrodelbahn**—One of the great Alpine experiences is to ride a chair lift up the mountain and "luge" down riding an oversized skateboard with brakes on a concrete bobsled course. On the Fernpass Road past the ruined castles on the way to Innsbruck are two luge courses. The first is ten minutes past the ruins—you'll see a chairlift on the right. Twenty minutes further toward Innsbruck, in Biberwier just past Lermoos (the first exit after a long tunnel, or, if you take the small road through Lermoos, turn left at the yellow skilift sign 50 yards before the Shell station), is a better luge, the longest in Austria—4,000 feet. Both are open 8:30-17:00, closed when wet. The concrete course banks on the corners and even a novice can go very very fast. No one emerges from this experience without a wind-blown hairdo and a smile-creased face.

Just before the longer luge is a great photo stop. Behind the sport and Trachtenstuberl shop is a wooden church dome with a striking Zugspitz backdrop. If you have sunshine and a camera, don't miss it.

▲▲ **Tyrolean Folk Evening**—The Tyroleans share their colorful folk dances, costumes, and traditions with visitors by putting on "folk evenings." Reutte has two or three a week and if you have the chance be sure to take one in. Your hotel will have the Reutte schedule of events and can call in a reservation for you. They usually start at 20:30 and cost 8 DM.

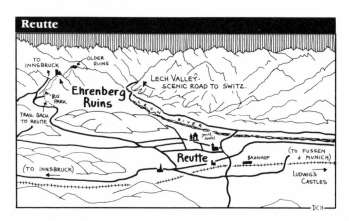

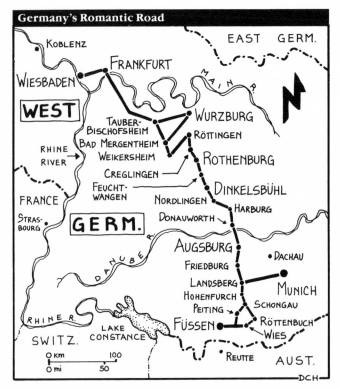

Germany's Romantic Road

Transportation

This is an easy day by car—no big cities, a scenic drive, and the border crossing is usually just a flash of the passport. By train or bus it's trickier. The Romantic Road bus gets into Fussen at 19:35, long after the last bus to Reutte. Eurailers will have an easier time riding the bus into Munich and doing Bavaria and Tyrol from there.

Food and Lodging

In July and August Munich and Bavaria are packed with tourists. Tyrol in Austria is easier and a bit cheaper. Reutte is just one of many good home base towns in the area. I choose it because it's not so crowded in peak season, the easy-going locals are always in a party mood, and I like to stay overnight in Austria.

  The tourist office should be your first stop in Reutte (one block in front of the station or "bahnhof," open Mon-Fri 8:00-12:00, 13:00-18:00, Sat 8:00-12:00, 16:00-18:00, Sun 16:00-18:00, tel 05672/2336 or direct from Germany

0043-5672/2336. They are very helpful and can always find you a cheap room ($8) in someone's home. Go over your plans with the T.I., see if they can book you a folk evening. Pick up a city map.

Reutte has a good little youth hostel (tel 05672-3039), and plenty of reasonable hotels and zimmers. For the youth hostel, follow the Jugendherberg signs from the town center, a 10-minute walk, non-members accepted, clean, rarely full, friendly, open only June 15-Aug 25. I stay at the big central **Hotel Goldener Hirsch** (from Germany dial 0043-5672-2508, in Ruette just the last four digits, ask for Helmut or Monika) which charges $18 per person and serves great $5 dinners.

In Munich there's a helpful room-finding service in the train station's tourist information office (open Mon-Sat 8:00-23:00, Sun 13:00-21:30, tel 239-1259). They can usually find you a reasonable room near the station. In Oberammergau I enjoyed friendly budget accommodations and hearty cooking at the **Gasthaus zum Stern** (Dorfstrasse 33, 8103 Oberammergau, tel 08822-867). They are closed Tuesdays and November, will hold a room with a phone call, speak English, 54 DM for a double. Oberammergau's youth hostel is unfriendly but very good in all other ways (tel 08822-4114). Countryside guest houses abound in Bavaria and are a great value. Look for signs that say "zimmer frei." The going rate is 42 DM per double including breakfast.

If Reutte isn't to your liking, nearby Lermoos and idyllic Nesselwangle are well zimmered. Fussen has lots of rooms— and many more tourists. The Bavarian countryside around Neuschwanstein is sprinkled with big farmhouse zimmers. You'll see plenty of green vacancy signs here.

While the cheapest food in Reutte is at the **SPAR** restaurant on Mullerstrasse near the station, the classy meals at **Hotel Goldener Hirsch** are not much more expensive. I like their huge "Gemuseplate" (vegetables) for 8 DM.

DAY 4

BAVARIA AND CASTLE DAY

Today we circle through the nutcracker and castle corner of
Bavaria. After touring Europe's most famous castle, Mad Ludwig's
Disney-esque Neuschwanstein, we'll visit Germany's most
ornate church, a Rococo riot. Next stop is Oberammergau,
Bavaria's wood carving capital and home of the famous passion
play, followed by another of Ludwig's extravagant castles—this
time the more liveable Linderhof Palace.

Suggested Schedule	
7:30	Breakfast.
8:15	Leave Reutte.
8:45	Tour Neuschwanstein Castle.
11:30	Picnic by the lake (Alpsee).
12:15	Drive to Wies church and on to Oberammergau.
1:45	Park at Passion Play Theater, take tour.
3:30	Tour Linderhof Castle (or shopping in Oberammergau).
5:00	Drive home to Reutte via Plansee.
8:30	Tyrolean Folk Evening (if not last night).
Sleep	Reutte

Transportation
This day is designed for drivers. Without your own wheels
it won't be possible. Transportation in the area is good but gaps
make the proposed circle impossible. Buses go from Reutte
to Fussen at 47 past each hour from 8:47 to 17:47. The 8:47 bus
goes straight to Ludwig's castle, but others stop at the Fussen
station where bus Bf-971 leaves hourly for the castle (2 DM).
The 55-minute train ride connects Munich and Fussen hourly.
Buses connect Fussen and Wieskirche only twice a day (6 DM).
The Reutte—Linderhof—Oberammergau bus leaves at 10:10,
stopping from 10:55 to 13:30 at Linderhof, arriving in Oberammergau at 13:55. At 15:10 a bus returns to Reutte getting in at
17:10. Trains connect Reutte and Garmish (7 a day, 1 hour) and
Innsbruck (6 a day, 2¾ hours). Hitchhiking is possible, but
instead I'd take an all-day bus tour from Munich to cover these
sights most efficiently.

Highlights of the Bavarian Circle
It's best to see Neuschwanstein, Germany's most popular castle,
early in the morning before the hordes hit. The castle is open

every morning at 8:30. By 10:00 it's packed. Hiking up the steep
road to the castle you may pass a crazy old bearded Bavarian.
(Hug him if you like, he's a photographer's feast, but women
beware of his infamous sauerkraut tongue). Take the English
tour and learn the story of Bavaria's Mad King Ludwig. The tour
is bare-boned and usually rushed. If possible, read up on
Wagner's operas and Ludwig's life before you visit.

After the tour, if you're energetic, climb up to Mary's Bridge
for a great view of Europe's "Disney" castle. The big yellow
more "lived-in" Hohenschwangau castle nearby was Ludwig's
boyhood home. Like its more exciting neighbor, its costs
about 6 DM and takes about an hour to tour.

Back down in the village you'll find several restaurants. The
self-service Braustuberl is the cheapest, with food that tastes
that way. Next door is a handy little grocery store. Picnic in
the lakeside park. At the intersection you'll find the best gift shop,
the bus stop, international dial-direct-to-home phone booths

Bavaria & Tyrol—The Castle Loop

(001-pause-area code-your number). Plug in one Deutsch
Mark for 15 seconds of hometown gossip.

Germany's greatest Rococo-style church, Wies Church, is
bursting with beauty just thirty minutes down the road. Go
north, turn right at Steingaden, and follow the signs. This
church is a droplet of heaven, a curly curlicue, the final flower-
ing of the Baroque movement. Read about it as you sit in its
splendor, then walk back to the car park the long way—
through the meadow.

Driving into Oberammergau, take the second left after crossing the river and park near the large modern Passion Play
Theater.

From Oberammergau drive through Garmisch, past Germany's
highest mountain, the Zugspitz, into Austria via Lermoos (and
the longest luge ride).

Or you can take the small scenic road past Ludwig's Linderhof
Castle. It's the most liveable palace I've seen. Incredible
grandeur on a homey scale and worth a look if you have the
energy and two hours for the tour. Wind past the windsurfer-
strewn Plansee, and back into Austria.

Sightseeing Highlights

▲▲▲ **Neuschwanstein**—This is the greatest of King Ludwig II
of Bavaria's fairly tale castles. His extravagance and romanticism
earned him the title "Mad King Ludwig." The obvious inspira-
tion of Disney's castle, it epitomizes the Romantic movement of
the 19th century. Set on a hilltop with a great view, it's decorated
inside and out with lavish damsels in distress, dragons, knights
in gleaming armor—respect for the good old Middle Ages.
Don't miss it—but miss the crowds by getting there early. Open
April-September 9:00-17:30, off season 10:00-16:00. The 6 DM
admission includes a mandatory (in English) tour. Often called
"Konigsschlosser" (Royal Castles) on maps, it's in the town of
Hohenschwangau, a five minute ride, not counting traffic jams,
from Fussen.

▲▲ **Hohenschwangau**—Much less spectacular and less
visited but more lived-in and giving a better look at Ludwig,
is his boyhood home castle, yellow and sitting just across the
ravine from Neuschwanstein (same hours).

▲▲▲ **Wies Church**—This lavish pilgrimage church set in a
peaceful meadow (Wies means meadow) is a must. Built by
Zimmerman in 1750, pilgrims and tourists from around the
world enjoy having their breath taken away here. Without a car,
it's not worth the headaches. See Wurzburg Chapel or Munich's
Asam Church instead.

▲▲ **Oberammergau**—This very touristy Shirley Temple of
Bavarian villages has found a need and filled it. If you like

buildings painted with scenery, fine wood carving, plenty of German cliches on sale and a chance to tour the great 5,000 seat Passion Play Spielhaus (theater), this is worth on hour or two.

Actually, the theater tour (2 DM, one hour tours throughout the day) is one-of-a-kind fascinating (next Passion Play is in 1990—watch out!). The carving shops are like wooden art galleries filled with very expensive whittled works. Visit the church, a cousin of the Wies, notice the Nazi tombstones in the graveyard—and get out.

▲▲ **Linderhof**—This is Mad Ludwig's "home," his most intimate castle, small and comfortably exquisite—enough for a minor god. Set in the woods, 15 minutes from Oberammergau,

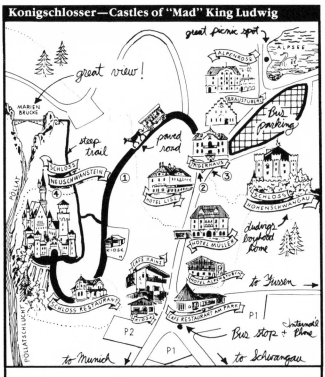

Konigschlosser—Castles of "Mad" King Ludwig

① "OLD BAVARIAN"- HUG HIM, BUT BEWARE OF HIS NOTORIOUS SAUERKRAUT TONGUE ☺

② BUS + HORSE CART STOP- FOR RIDE UP TO CASTLE - ITS A 20 MIN WALK.

③ SMALL GROCERY STORE

④ SCENIC TRAIL DOWN POLLAT GORGE - GORGEOUS!

surrounded by fountains and sculpted, Italian style gardens, it's
the only palace I've toured that actually had me feeling envious.
Don't miss the grotto. Open April-Sept, 9:00-17:00, off season
9:00-16:00, July and Aug til 17:30. English tours constantly. Plan
to stop for two hours. There's a fair amount of walking.

▲ **Tegelberg Gondola**—Just north of Neuschwanstein, for 10
DM this lift will carry you high above the castle to that peak's
5,500-foot summit. On a clear day you get great views of the
Alps and Bavaria and the thrill of watching hang gliders leap into
airborne ecstasy. From there it's a lovely 2-hour hike to Ludwig's castle. Tegelberg has a mountain hut with Tolkien atmosphere and 10 DM beds if you'd like to spend the night and do
Ludwig's place the next morning. (Last ride is at 17:00).

Swimming Pool—Reutte has an Olympic-quality swimming
pool open from 10:00 to 21:00 which might be a good way to
cool off after your castle hikes.

▲▲ **Fallerscheim**—A special treat for those who may have
been Kit Carson in a previous life, this extremely remote log
cabin village smothered in Alpine goodness is a flower-speckled
world of serene slopes, cowbells, river and breeze music.
Thunderstorms roll down this valley like it's God's bowling
alley, but the pint-sized church on the high ground, blissfully
simple after so much Baroque, seems to promise this huddle of
houses will remain standing. The people sitting on benches are
mostly Austrian vacationers who've rented cabins here. For a
rugged chunk of local Alpine peace, spend a night in the local
Matratzenlager (simple loft dorm) "Almwirtscheft Fallerscheim"
run by friendly (but no English spoken) Kerle Erwin, open
June-Sept, 6 DM per night, 27 beds, one outhouse, good 8 DM
meals, 6671 Weissenbach 119a, b/Reutte, tel 05678-5142.
Crowded only on weekends. Fallerscheim (at 4,000 feet altitude) is at the end of a miserable 2-mile fit-for-jeep-or-rental-
car-only gravel road near Namlose on the Berwang road
south of Reutte.

Itinerary Options

Train travelers may prefer doing "castle day" as a side trip from
Munich. Organized tours do the Bavarian biggies in a day (the
Grey Line, tel 5904-248, does Neuschwanstein, Linderhof,
Oberammergau, and the Wies Church in a busy ten hour day
for 46 DM, departing daily at 8:30 from near the Munich station). Staying in Reutte may not be worth the transportation
headaches for those without wheels.

Remember, the luge experience is possible only on dry days.
It fits easily into Day 3, 4, or 5.

If you're skipping Vienna, do Munich first, then Reutte, then
follow the lovely Lech River valley into Switzerland.

DAY 5
REUTTE TO MUNICH

Today we'll drive past Germany's highest peak, possibly stopping for a little more Bavarian sightseeing and lunch at a monastery that serves the best beer in Deutschland and then arriving in Munich in time to set up, orient, see the center of Bavaria's leading city and enjoy some beerhall fun tonight.

Munich, Germany's most liveable city, is also one of its most historic, artistic, and entertaining. It's big and growing—with a population of over 1,500,000. Just a little more than a century ago, it was the capital of an independent Bavaria. Its imperial palaces, jewels, and grand boulevards constantly remind visitors that this was once a political as well as cultural powerhouse.

Suggested Schedule

8:00	Leave Reutte.
9:00	Ride to the summit of the Zugspitz if weather and budget permit.
11:00	Drive to Andechs for lunch. Be very beerful.
14:00	Arrive in Munich, stop at T.I., and check into hotel.
15:30	Explore the heart of town, subway to Odeonsplatz, tour Cuvillies Theater, see 17:00 glockenspiel at Marienplatz, shopping, browsing, stroll through center, drop into Hofbrauhaus.
20:00	Dinner and evening of oom-pah fun at Mauthaser's beer hall.
Sleep	Munich.

Sightseeing Highlights
▲▲ **Zugspitz**—Germany's tallest mountain, 10,000 feet, is on the Austrian border. Lifts from both sides take you to the summit where you can mingle back and forth over the border enjoying an incredible view. There are restaurants, shops, telescopes, etc. on top. The lift from the German side departs hourly, takes 75 minutes, costs 44 DM. From the "Talstation Obermoos," above the Austrian village of Erwald, it's faster, 20% cheaper, and less crowded, but is tricky without your own car. The old gondola (built it 1926—notice the historic displays) leaves every seven minutes and if you have a sunny day, 30 DM, and 90 extra minutes, the Tiroler Zugspitzbahn is worthwhile.

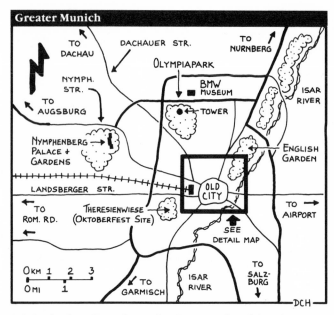

▲▲ Andechs—How does a fine Baroque church in a Bavarian
setting at a monastery that serves hearty food and the best beer
in Germany in a carnival setting full of partying locals sound?
That's the soon-to-be-discovered Andechs monastery hiding
happily between two lakes just south of Munich. Come with an
appetite—the food is great—chunks of tender pork chain-
sawed especially for you, huge and soft pretzels (best I've had),
spiralled white radishes, savory sauerkraut, and Andecher beer
that lives up to its reputation. Everything is served in medieval
proportions—two people can split a meal. Great picnic center,
too. Open daily 9:00-21:00, second class prices, first class view.
Munich Sights—See tomorrow's listing.
Overrated Sights—The Ettal monastery is just another pretty
Baroque face with a knack for commercialism. Garmisch-
Partenkirchen is worth stopping at only if you're in the US
Army and have no choice.

Munich Orientation
If you stop at Andechs, a small road takes you into town. Otherwise you'll autobahn from Garmisch. Follow signs to "Zentrum" and "Hauptbahnhof." Munich is a terrible city to drive in,
so ideally, you'll go straight to the station, find your room
within a few blocks of there, leave your car until it's time to go

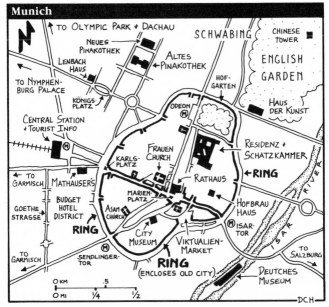

to Salzburg when you'll head out the way you came in, following the Salzburg autobahn signs.

Munich is big—Germany's third largest city—and growing fast, but its excellent tourist information and sleek subway system make life easy for the 5 million visitors who come to town each year.

Take full advantage of the T.I. in the train station (open 8:00-23:00 daily, tel 239-1259, opposite track 11). Have a list of questions ready, confirm your sightseeing plans, and pick up brochures (30 pf city map, how to use the public transit, lists of sights, calendar of events, and the young people's guide—get one regardless of your age). If necessary, take advantage of their room finding service. For recorded museum info call 239174, and for sights info: 239175. Train info: 592991.

The great Munich tram, bus, and subway system is a sight in itself. Subways are called U- or S-bahns. Eurail passes are good on the S-bahn. The fares are complicated and three rides will cost you the same as a 24-hour pass so spend 6.50 DM, sign it, validate it in a machine and you have Munich by the tail for a day (on sale at tourist offices, subway booths and in machines at most stops). The entire system works on the same tickets. Taxis are very expensive and needless.

Orient yourself in Munich with the Hauptbahnhof—Karlstor—Kaufingerstrasse—Marienplatz—Isartor axis. Most sights are within a few blocks of this lovely walk.

You'll find Munich a bit sterile since most of it, including many of the historic buildings, has been rebuilt since the WWII bombings. Its hotels are expensive, but after that, food, fun, and transportation are cheap.

City telephone code is 089. From Austria dial 050/49/89/and the local number. Most Munich sights are closed on Mondays.

Food and Lodging

Rooms in Munich are expensive—you can't avoid it. Youth hostels strictly enforce their 26-year-old age limit and side-tripping in is a bad value. But there are plenty of good rooms, most located within a few blocks of the Hauptbahnhof (central train station) with its excellent room finding service. Ideally, call ahead and reserve one of the places I've listed below. Otherwise, use the T.I.

The info people hate the word "cheap." They recommend rooms selectively and can normally get mid-day arrivals an 80 DM double in a pension. The best budget rooms are near the station. Evening arrivals may be stuck in a 110 DM hotel room. Even dorm flophouses cost well over 20 DM per person.

Hotel Gebhardt on Goethestrasse 38, 8000 Munich 2, just three minutes from the station was the best combination of neighborhood, comfort, and price I could find. 65 DM doubles, English spoken, tel 089/539446 or 539585. With shower, 95 DM, some cheaper 3- and 4-bed rooms.

Pension Monopteros on Oettingenstrasse 35, overlooking the Englischer Garten is not so central but more peaceful. On a tram line, simple, friendly, tel 292348, 100 DM doubles.

International Haus on Elisabethstrasse 87, tel 089/185081 offers 600 beds in depressing 5-bed rooms. 27 DM per person, they'll hold a room with a phone call, normally has beds available. Easy to find, easy parking.

Jugendhotel Marienherberg is a very pleasant, friendly convent accepting young women only (18-25 year age limit) charging 25 DM per person in 5-bed rooms. Very close to station at Goethestrasse 9, tel 089/555891.

YMCA (CVJM) is open to people of all ages and sexes. Very central, just two blocks south of the station at Landwehrstrasse 13, tel 089/555941, charging about 32 DM per person in a double, this is a great bet if you can get a spot.

Munich's Youth Hostels charge about 16 DM, and strictly limit admission to YH members who are under 27. If you qualify, call 723650 or 7236550.

"The Tent," Munich's International Youth Camp "Kapuzinerholzl" offers a place on the wooden floor of a huge circus tent with a mattress, blankets, good showers, and free tea in the morning for 5 DM to anyone under 23. It's a fun experience—kind of a cross between Woodstock (if anyone under 23 knows what that was) and a slumber party. Call 1414300 before heading out. No curfew. Take the U-bahn 1 to Rotkreuzplatz, catch streetcar 12 to Botanischer Garten, and follow the youthful crowd down Franz-Schrankstrasse to the big tent. This is near the Nymphenburg palace. Open from the end of June through August.

The best budget food in Munich is in the beerhalls. There are many to choose from but I'm stuck on the **Mauthaser Bierstadt** at 5 Bayerstrasse halfway between the Hauptbahnhof (train station) and Karlstor. The atmosphere is thick, the fat and shiny-leather band has even church mice standing up and conducting ¾ time with a breadstick. Meals cost 10 DM (I like the schweinwurst and kraut), huge liter beers (called "ein Mass") are 6 DM, white radishes are salted and cut in delicate spirals and huge beermaids pull mustard packets from their cavernous cleavages.

The most famous beerhall, the **Hofbrauhaus**, is much more touristy. But dew-drop in—it's fun to see 200 Japanese drinking beer in a German beerhall. Many beerhalls are closed Mondays.

For outdoor atmosphere and a cheap meal, spend an evening at the **Englischer Garten's Chinese Pagoda** bierstadt. You're welcome to BYO Food and grab a table or buy from picnic stall ("brotziet") right there. 6,000 seats!

For university atmosphere, cheap food, beer and crowded basements of conversation, head out to the **Studentenstadt** (University dorm) bierstuben.

The fastest cheap and central meal is found at **Mauthaser's** stand-up self-serve bar (facing Bayerstrasse) or at the lively open-air **Viktualien Market**, just behind Marienplatz. Plenty of good picnic material here.

The classiest picnic of the tour can be purchased in the historic elegant—and expensive—**Alois Dallmayr** delicatessen at 15 Dienerstrasse just behind the Rathaus. Wander through this dieter's purgatory, put together a royal picnic and eat it in the nearby, and adequately royal, Hofgarten. To save money, browse at Dallmayr's but buy in the basement of the Kaufhof across Marienplatz.

DAY 6

MUNICH

We'll spend all day immersed in the art and history of this
cultural hub of Germany. To see this exciting Bavarian capital in
less than two days requires selectivity and careful planning.
Today will include a mountain of Baroque razzle-dazzle, crown
jewels, great art and biergarten fun.

Suggested Schedule	
8:00	Breakfast.
9:00	Munchner Statmuseum, Viktualien market (buy picnic here or at Alois Dallmayr).
11:00	Tour Residenz and Shatzkammer.
12:30	Picnic in Hofgarten, walk to Alte Pinakothek.
13:30	Alte Pinakothek.
15:30	Haus der Kunst or free time.
17:00	Stroll through Englischer Garten, early dinner or a drink at the Chinese Pagoda.

Sightseeing Highlights

▲▲ **Marienplatz and the Pedestrian Zone**—The essence of
Munich is best experienced as the escalator takes you out of the
underground system and into the sunlit Marienplatz. Surrounding you is the glory of Munich—great buildings bombed flat
and rebuilt—the ornate facades of the new and old City Halls
(Altes Rathaus), outdoor cafes, and people bustling and linger-
ing like the birds and breeze they share this square with. From
here the pedestrian mall (Kaufingerstrasse and
Neuhauserstrasse) leads you through a great shopping area past
plenty of fun street singers, the towering Frauenkirche (with
its 350-foot high viewpoint), and several fountains, to Karlstor
and the train station. The old glockenspiel "jousts" as it has for
generations on Marienplatz daily at 11:00, 12:00 and 17:00.
(If you liked the Rothenburg Meistertrunk show, you'll love
this one!)

▲▲ **Residenz**—For a good dose of imperial Bavarian grandeur,
tour the palace of the Wittelsbach family. Different wings are
open in the morning and afternoon but either tour is ample. For
600 years the Wittelsbachs ruled Bavaria from here. Don't miss
the Schatzkammer (treasury), a thousand years of Wittelsbach
heirlooms, which, like the palace, is open Tues-Sat 10:00-16:30,
Sun 10:00-13:00. Take U-3, or 6 to Odeonsplatz or walk from
Mary's Place.

▲▲ **The Cuvillies Theater**—Attached to the Residenz, this National Theater, designed by Cuvillies is dazzling enough to send you back to the days of the divine monarch. Open Mon-Sat 14:00-17:00, Sun 10:00-17:00.

▲ **Munchner Stadtmuseum**—The underrated Munich city museum just a few blocks off Marienplatz is a pleasant surprise—great old photography exhibit, historic puppets, the story of beer, the world's largest collection of musical instruments and the best collection of Jugendstil art (Art Nouveau) I've seen. Bored and very playful guards, no crowds. Open 9:00-16:30, closed Mondays.

▲▲ **Alte Pinakothek**—Bavaria's best collection of art, stored in a pleasing easy-to-handle museum. Strong on Italian and North European artists, Durer and Rubens. Open 9:00-16:30, closed Monday, open 19:00-21:00 on Tues and Thurs. Take U-8 to Konigsplatz.

▲ **Haus der Kunst**—Built by Hitler as a temple of Nazi art, this bold and fascist building now houses modern art—much of which the Fuhrer censored. It's a fun collection—Kandinsky, Picasso, Dali, and much more from this century. Open 9:00-16:30, closed Mondays. Take U-3, 5 or 6 to Odeonsplatz and a peaceful walk through the Hofgarten and past the "Krieger-denkmal"—a bombed building left as a war memorial. (Or, take bus 53, 55, or Tram 20.)

Bayerisches Nationalmuseum—An interesting collection of Riemenschneider carvings, manger scenes, traditional living rooms and old Bavarian houses. Open 9:00-17:00, closed Mondays. Take tram 20, bus 53 or 55.

▲ **Deutsches Museum**—This German answer to our Smith-sonian Museum has everything of scientific and technical interest from astronomy to zymurgy. This museum can be disappointing due to its overwhelming size and lack of English descriptions. Pick up the 4 DM "guide through the collections," skip the German-only planetarium, and focus on the lower floors where you'll find more English info. With ten miles of exhibits you'll need to be selective. Lots of hands-on gadgetry but the collections seem to have been left in the dust by the computer age. Self-serve cafeteria. Open 9:00-17:00, 5 DM admission. S-Bahn to Isartorplatz or tram 18. Despite its reputation, unless you are (or wish you were) an engineer, two hours is enough time here.

Schwabing—Munich's artsy and Bohemian university district or "Greenwich Village" has been called "not a place but a state of mind." That may have been a compliment but all I experienced was a mental lapse. The Bohemians run the boutiques and I think the most colorful thing about Schwabing is the road leading back downtown. U-3 or 6 will take you to the Mun-chener-Freiheit Center if you want to wander. The most jazz and disco joints are near Occamstrasse.

▲ **Englischer Garten**—One of Europe's great parks, this "Central Park" of Munich is the Continent's largest, laid out in 1789 by an American. Bike rentals are at the south entrance, and there's a huge beer garden near the Chinese Pagoda. Caution: nude sunbathers. A very rewarding respite from the city.

Asam Church—Near the Stadtmuseum, this private church of the Asam brothers shows off their very popular Baroque-con-centrate style. If you missed (or loved) the Wies Church, visit the masterpiece by these two Rococonuts. It has been said that we get our word "awesome" from the gooey drippy style of these architects.

▲ **Olympic Grounds**—Munich's great 1972 Olympic stadium and sports complex is now a fine park offering a tower (com-manding but rather boring view, 8:00-24:00, 4 DM), excellent swimming pool (open to the public 7:00-22:00, Mondays 10:00-22:00, 4 DM), a good look at its striking "cobweb" style of architecture, and plenty of sun, grass and picnic potential. Easy access on the U-3 or 8 to Olympiazentrum.

BMW Museum—Fascinating only to yuppies or those who are into cars, the BMW headquarters, located in a striking building across the street from the Olympic Grounds, offers free factory tours and a museum. Sign up for an English tour and spend your wait touring the museum.

▲▲ **Nymphenburg Palace**—This royal summer palace is mediocre if you've already seen the Residenz. If you do tour it don't miss King Ludwig's "Gallery of Beauties"—a room stacked with portraits of Bavaria's loveliest women—according to Lud-wig. (Notice his taste for big noses). The palace park, good for a royal stroll, contains the tiny Amalienburg palace, a Rococo jewel of a hunting lodge by Cuvillies. The sleigh and coach collection (Marstallmuseum) is especially interesting for Mad Ludwig fans. The palace cafeteria is reasonably priced. Open 9:00-12:30, 13:30-17:00, closed Mondays, shorter hours Oct-March. Admission 5 DM, use the 2.50 DM English guide-book. Take the U-1 and then tram 12 toward Amalienburg-strasse, to Schloss Nymphenburg.

▲▲ **Dachau**—Since we plan to visit the even more powerful Mauthausen concentration camp, I haven't worked Dachau into our schedule. But if you won't be touring Mauthausen on your way to Vienna, please visit Dachau. Dachau was the first Nazi concentration camp (1933). Today it is the most accessible camp to travelers and is a very effective voice from our recent but grisly past, warning and pleading "Never Again"—the memorial's theme. This is a valuable experience, and when approached thoughtfully is well worth the drive—in fact, it may change your life. See it. Feel it. Read and think about it. After this most powerful sightseeing experience, many people gain a respect for history and are inspired to learn more about contemporary injustices, and work against tragic reccurences.

Upon arrival, pick up the mini-guide and notice when the next documentary film in English will be shown (normally at 11:30 and 15:30). The museum and the movie are worthwhile. Notice the Expressionist fascist-inspired art near the theater. Outside, be sure to tour the reconstructed barracks and the memorial shrines at the far end. (Near the theater are English books, slides and a good w.c. The camp is open 9:00-17:00, closed on Mondays).

Take the S-bahn 2 to Dachau and catch bus 722 (Dachau-Ost) from the station to Gedenkstatte. If you're driving, Dachauerstrasse leads from downtown Munich to Dachau, follow the K2—Gedenkstatte signs. Open Tues-Sun 9:00-17:00. (Note: train travelers should see Dachau rather than Mauthausen.)

Octoberfest—While you can always find a festival in Munich's beerhalls, the entire city celebrates each fall with this greatest of beer parties. Starting the third Saturday of every September and roasting the last ox two weeks later, this mammoth festival is an experience of a lifetime. It's crowded, but arrive in the morning and the T.I. will find you a room. The fairgrounds known as the "Wies'n" (a few blocks from the station) erupt in a frenzy of rides, dancing, strangers strolling arm in arm down rows of picnic tables, and tons of beer, pretzels and wurst in a bubbling cauldron of fun. The "three loops" roller-coaster must be the greatest on earth (do it *before* the beerdrinking). During the fair, the city functions even better than normal and it's a good time to sightsee even if beerhall rowdiness isn't your cup of tea. The Fasching carnival time before Lent is nearly as wild.

DAY 7

MUNICH TO SALZBURG

After a free morning to do any last sightseeing or exploring in Munich, we'll autobahn two hours south back into Austria, setting up in Salzburg by mid-afternoon. Today's sightseeing plan is flexible. There are four major sights and you must pick two—the Nymphenburg Palace and the Deutsches Museum in Munich and the Berchtesgaden Salt Mines and the Hellbrunn castle near Salzburg. Speedsters with a car could do three but I'd rather do two and get comfortably set up to take a rest before a hopefully music-filled Salzburg evening.

Suggested Schedule	
9:00	Check out of hotel. Tour Nymphenburg Palace or the Deutsches Museum.
11:30	Drive south, picnicking en route.
14:00	Tour the Berchtesgaden salt mines or the Hellbrunn castle.
17:00	Arrive in Salzburg, visit T.I., check into hotel.
19:30	Stroll through gardens to Augustiner Keller for dinner, floodlit city-from-the-bridge view for dessert.
22:00	Wander the streets of old Salzburg.

AUSTRIA

32,000 square miles (South Carolina's size).
7.6 million people (235 per square mile and holding).
One Shilling = 7 cents, 15 AS = $1

Austria during the grand old Hapsburg days, was Europe's most powerful empire. Its royalty put together that giant empire of more than 50 million people by making love, not war—having lots of children and marrying them into the other royal houses of Europe.

Today Austria is a small landlocked country that does more to cling to its elegant past than any other in Europe. The waltz is still the rage and Austrians are very sociable. More so than anywhere else, it's important to greet people you pass on the streets or meet in shops. The Austrian's version of "Hi" is a cheerful "Gruss, Gott!" (May God be with you). You'll get the correct pronunciation after the first volley—listen and copy.

While they speak German and German money is readily ac-

cepted in Salzburg, Innsbruck and Reutte, the Austrians cherish
their distinct cultural and historical traditions. They are not
Germans. Austria is mellow and relaxed compared to Deutschland. "Gemutlichkeit" is the special local word for this special
Austrian cozy-and-easy approach to life. It's good living—
either engulfed in mountain beauty or swirling in high culture.
The people like to stroll as if every day were Sunday, topping
things off with a visit to a coffee or pastry shop. It must be nice
to be past your prime—no longer troubled by being powerful,
able to kick back and enjoy just being happy in the clean, un-
troubled mountain air.

While the Austrians make less money per year than their
neighbors, they work less (34 hours a week) and live longer (14
percent of the people are senior citizens, the highest percentage
in the world). Austria is technically part of Eastern Europe and
therefore not in NATO or the EEC.

Austrians eat on about the same schedule as we do. Treats
include Wiener Schnitzel (breaded veal cutlet), Knodel (dumplings), Apfelstrudel and fancy desserts. White wines, Heuriger
(new wine) and coffee are delicious and popular. Shops are
open from 8 am-5 pm. Banks keep roughly the same hours, but
usually close for lunch.

Transportation
By car leave Munich the way you came in, heading away from
town on Bayerstrasse and following the autobahn signs to
Salzburg—just 60 miles to the southeast. You'll pass Herren-
chiemsee or your left and the very first autobahn reststop built
during Hitler's rule and frescoed with "Deutschland uber alles"
themes (take the Feldon exit, presently a lakeside U.S. military
hotel). After crossing the border stay on the autobahn curving
south in the direction of Hallein before taking the Salzburg exit

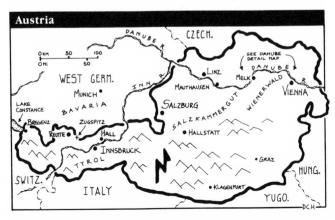

at Anif. This road leads you north into town passing first the
Schloss Hellbrunn and then the Tourist Info. Ask the T.I. for advice on locating your hotel and parking. Don't even try to drive
in the old town. Park your car and walk or use the bus system.

By train it's an easy 90-minute shot to Salzburg. Use the
Salzburg station T.I. and catch a city bus from there to Hellbrunn if you like (Bus H, departing at 10 and 40 past each hour,
12 AS, 15-minute ride). For Berchtesgaden, take the train direct
from Munich, easy and scenic bus connection into Salzburg.

Sightseeing Highlights
▲ **Berchtesgaden**—This Alpine resort flaunts its attractions
very effectively and you may find yourself in a traffic jam of
desperate tourists looking for ways to turn their money into
fun. From the station and the helpful T.I. (tel 08652/5011) buses
go to the idyllic Konigsee (2-hour scenic cruises, 15 DM) and
the salt mine (a 30-minute walk otherwise).

The salt mines—the best of four regional mines I've toured—
are open daily 8:00-17:00 (winter, Mon-Fri 12:30-15:30). For 12
DM you put on the traditional miners' outfits, get on funny little
trains and go zipping deep into the mountain. For 90 minutes
you'll cruise subterranean lakes, slide speedily down long
wooden (splinter-free) bannisters, and learn how they mined
salt so long ago.

Hitler's famous "eagle's nest" towered high above Berchtesgaden. Now Kehlstein and Obersalzburg are open to visitors but
little of Hitler's Alpine retreat remains (he only went there five
times) and the ride up the private road costs about 16 DM. The
view is great but I'd skip it.
▲ **Hellbrunn Castle**—The real attraction here is a garden of
clever trick fountain and the sadistic joy the tour guide gets
by soaking the tourists in his group. The archbishop's palace is
hardly worth a look, his garden is pretty enough, but bring a
raincoat and dive into the bubbly tour. Open 9:00-17:30 daily,
6 DM for the tour, three miles south of Salzburg just off the road
as you enter, or bus H from downtown.
Salzburg Sights—See Tomorrow.

Salzburg Orientation
Salzburg, with a well-preserved old town, gardens, churches,
lush surroundings, set under Europe's biggest intact medieval
castle and forever smiling to the tunes of Mozart and The Sound
of Music, is a town that knows how to be popular.

This city of 140,000 is divided into old and new. The old
town sitting between two hills straddling the river holds all the
charm and is served by a fine bus system (12 AS/ride, 3 rides =
the cost of a 24 hour pass). The T.I. office (at the train station,

on Mozartplatz in the old center, and on the freeway entrance to the city) is your essential first stop. When you arrive at the T.I., get a room, confirm your plans, and have your list of questions answered. Ask for a map, sights list, youth in Salzburg booklet, and a schedule of events. Try to book a concert for this evening. If you missed the folk evening in Reutte, you may catch one tonight.

Food and Lodging
Finding a room in Salzburg—even during the Music Festival—is easy. The tourist offices can give you a pamphlet listing all the pensions, hostels, and private rooms in town, or they can find you a 20 DM bed in the neighborhood of your choice.

Zimmers, or private rooms, abound. They cost about 20 DM per person and are cozy but normally far from the center. Use the T.I.

Salzburg's **youth hostels** are excellent and have no age limit. Call 75030 (July and Aug), 842670 (all year), 76241 (April-Sept). Most charge about 90 AS and start checking in at 17:00 (see appendix).

Institute St. Sebastian—It's usually easy to get a room here. Friendly, clean, great historic location next to graveyard with Mozart's mom, $25 doubles, $10 per dorm bed, breakfast extra, those with sheets save 15 AS. Will hold a room with a phone call. On Linzer Gasse 41, directly across river from the old town. Tel. 71386.

Zum Junger Fuchs—Great location, funky old building, cheap, plain, elderly management 300 AS doubles, no breakfast, showers extra. Across from Institute St. Sebastian at Linzer Gasse 54, tel 75496.

Salzburg boasts many fun and atmospheric places to eat. My favorite is the **Augustiner Braustuble** at Augustinergasse 4 (walk through the Mirabellgarten, over the Mullnersteg bridge and ask for help). This place is so rustic and crude that I hesitate to show my true colors by recommending it but I must. It's like a Munich beerhall without the music, a historic setting with beer-sloshed smoke-stained halls, and a pleasant outdoor beer garden serving another fine local monastic brew. Local students mix with tourists here eating hearty slabs of schnitzel with their fingers or cold meals from the picnic counter. 1,000 seats, open daily 15:00-23:00. It'll bring out the barbarian in you. For dessert enjoy the incomparable floodlit view from the nearby pedestrian bridge. More central and normal (and not as fun) is the **Stiftskeller St. Peter** or **Peterkeller** next to St Peter's church and Mouchsberg.

DAY 8

SALZBURG AND THE SALZKAMMERGUT

Today we'll enjoy the sights of Salzburg and spend the afternoon in Sound of Music country—the Salzkammergut Lake
District—spending the night in the postcard pretty fjord-
cuddling town of Hallstatt.

Suggested Schedule	
9:00	Tour Hohensalzburg—the castle.
10:45	Visit Glockenspiel as it performs or tour festival houses.
12:00	Picnic, check out of hotel.
14:00	Drive into Lakes District.
	Afternoon and evening free in Hallstatt (or Eurailers will stay in Salzburg and take 14:00 Sound of Music Tour for a look at the lakes).
Sleep	Hallstatt.

Transportation
Everything in Salzburg today can be done on foot. When you're
ready to depart, by car leave Salzburg on the Grazer Bundes-
strasse (up Linzer Gasse, over the tracks, right on Minnesheim-
strasse, and wind out of town following signs to Gaisberg,
Fuschlsee, and St Gilgen). A detour up the Gaisberg takes you to
a 3,800-foot summit and a good view. Soon the "hills are alive"
and you're surrounded by the loveliness that has turned on
everyone from Emperor Franz Josef to Julie Andrews. This is the
Sound of Music country (alias the Salzkammergut Lake District).

The road to Hallstatt leads past St Gilgen (pleasant but touristy) to Bad Ischl, the center of the Salzkammergut (with a spa,
salt mine tour, casino, and good tourist office tel 06132-3520),
a tiny 600-year-old roadside watermill just north of the town of
Au (worth a look), and along Hallstattersee to Hallstatt. Park in
the middle of the tunnel, you'll see a "P" sign and a waterfall.
Walk down into town from there. This lot is free, affords a fine
view of the town and lake, and parking in town is frustrating.

While the Salzkammergut is well served by trains and buses,
I'd recommend that Eurailers see it from the window of the
Sound of Music tour (described later), spend the night in Salzburg again and take the early train toward Vienna. If you do take
the time to train into the Salzkammergut, the ride to Hallstatt
is gorgeous and the thrilling finale is a boat ride that connects
the town with its station across the lake.

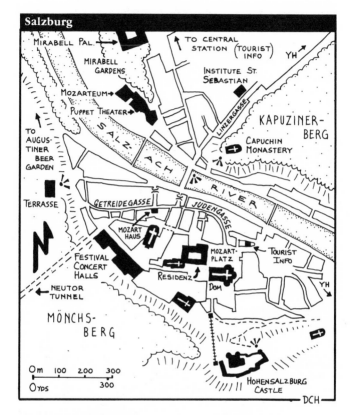

Sightseeing Highlights

▲▲ Fortress Hohensalzburg—This castle so dominates Salzburg's skyline that a visit is almost required. The interior is so-so and the tour not worth your time. But the view is great and it's fun to romp around Europe's greatest medieval fortress. The funicular will zip you effortlessly to the top (21 AS round-trip, rides leave constantly). Open daily, 10 AS entrance, 30 AS with tour.

▲ City Walking Tour—A great one hour 50 AS guided walking tour of the old town leaves from the T.I. at Mozartplatz daily at 12:15 (May-October).

▲▲ Sound of Music Tour—I took this tour skeptically (as part of my research chores) and was very impressed. It includes a quick but good general city tour, hits all the S.O.M. spots (including the gazebo, the stately home and the wedding church), and shows you a lovely stretch of the Salzkammergut. The

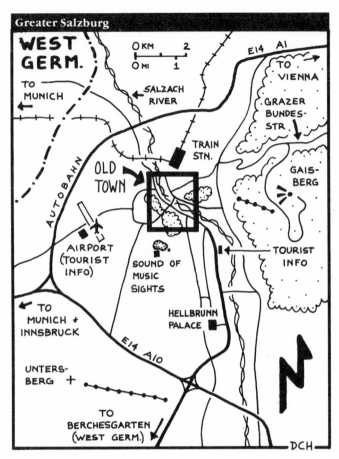

Greater Salzburg

Salzburg Panorama Tours Company charges 220 AS for the 3½
hour tour which leaves from Mirabellplatz daily at 9:30 and
14:00. Telephone 74029 for a reservation and a free hotel
pickup if you like. This is worthwhile for S.O.M. fans without
a car or who won't otherwise be going into the Salzkammergut.
Warning: The bus is entirely full of Americans singing "Do—
a Deer," and "Climb Every Mountain."

▲▲▲ **Salzburg Festival**—Each summer from late July to early
September, Salzburg hosts its famous Salzburger Festspiele. This
is a fun and festive time to be in Salzburg and, while it's crowded, there are plenty of beds and usually some tickets available
the day of the concert. Salzburg is busy with concerts in its
palaces and churches year round and if you want music, this
is the place to come.

▲ **Mozart's Birthplace (Geburtshaus)**—Maybe it's just me, but I find birthplaces of famous people are usually as dead as they are. This is almost a pilgrimage though, and if you loved Amadeus you'll have to check it out. Right in the old town on colorful Getreidegasse, open daily 9:00-19:00, 30 AS.

▲ **Getreidegasse**—Old Salzburg's main drag, this is a very lively and colorful street famous for its many old guild signs, and still looking much like it did in Mozart's day.

▲ **Carillon**—The bell tower on Mozartplatz chimes throughout the day. The man behind the bells gives fascinating tours on weekdays at 10:45 and 17:45. You'll actually be up on top among 35 bells as the big barrel turns, the music flies, and you learn what a "dingbat" is. Buy your 10 AS tickets 10 minutes early.

▲ **Festival Houses**—The great concert halls of the Salzburg festival offer tours at 11:00 and 15:00 Mon-Fri except during the festival. Worthwhile.

▲ **Mirabell Gardens and Palace (Schloss)**—The gardens are always open and free but to really enjoy the lavish palace try to get a ticket to a concert in the "Mirabellschloss"—Baroque music contained in a Baroque hall is a happy bird in the right cage. Tickets are around $15 (students, half price) and rarely sold out.

▲▲ **Salzkammergut**—This is Austria's commune with nature country. Idyllic, magestic, but not rugged. It's a land of lakes, forested mountains, storybook villages, endless hiking opportunities, and plenty of cheap private homes and youth hostels. While you could easily zimmer down here and make this area the focus of your trip we are just sneaking it in quickly, content to get in a representative taste and a very pleasant and restful evening.

▲▲▲ **Hallstatt**—Our target is Hallstatt—a town whose photograph always draws desirous gasps when I show it to my travel classes. Hallstatt is tiny, bullied onto a ledge by a selfish mountain and a lovely lake. It can be toured on foot in about 10 minutes.

The T.I. (tel 06134-208, daily 9:30-16:30) can find you a room and point you wherever you'd like. The humble museum adjacent to the T.I. is interesting since little Hallstatt was the center of this part of Europe in 1000 B.C. Celtic tribes dug for precious salt here and there have been many interesting finds here from what archeologists all over the world call the "Hallstatt Period."

The church cemetery in town is so old that the bones of the long dead had to make way for the newly dead. The result is a fascinating chapel of bones. This is the only opportunity bone fans will have on this tour to see the real thing.

The nearby Dachstein Caves are famous but not worth our time or money. The Hallstatt salt mine tour is fun but tedious. You'll ride a frighteningly steep funicular high above the town, take a short hike, do the same old miners' clothes underground train routine as at Berchtesgaden and listen to a German-only tour. The publicized ancient Celtic graveyard excavation sites are a real disappointment.

The charm of Hallstatt is the village and lakeside setting. Go there to relax, eat, walk, and paddle. Note: In August tourist crowds trample most of Hallstatt's charm.

Lodging
The T.I. can almost always find you a room. Only August—especially the first two weeks—is bad. There are plenty of zimmers generally charging 150 AS/night. Some will charge quite a bit more for stays less than three nights.

Gasthoff Simony—My favorite, with a lake view, balconies, creaky wood floors, antique furniture, stocking-feet tidy, right on the square, 380 AS per double. Call Susan Scheutz at 06134/231 for a reservation. Address: 4830 Hallstatt.

Pension Sarstein—At Gosaumuhlstrasse 83, tel 217, good central location with a view, 150 AS/person.

The Nature Freunde-Herberge—At Kirchenweg 36 just below the car park, tel 318, but absolutely no English spoken, 100 AS per person in 6-bed rooms. Open all year, a good value. ("Nature's friends houses" are found throughout the Alps. Like our Mountaineers' huts, they are cheap, good, fun and basic).

The Youth Hostel—On Salzbergstrasse just below the salt mine lift, clean, very simple, 40 AS, tel 681 or 279. Open May 15-Sept 15.

The nearby village of Obertraun is a peaceful alternative to Hallstatt in August. You'll find plenty of zimmers and a luxurious youth hostel.

Itinerary Options
Two nights in a row in Salzburg with the S.O.M. bus tour for a look at the lakes district is best for Eurailers. But if you're feeling good and energetic, try to spend the night in Hallstatt. If you prefer rivers to lakes and have had enough of Salzburg by noon, hit the road for the Danube River valley and spend the evening in a whole different, more eastern-feeling world on a river that could float you all the way to Russia.

DAY 9
HALLSTATT TO VIENNA

Today we head to our tour's easternmost point, traveling as quickly as possible to the Danube River where we'll tour the powerful Mauthausen concentration camp and explore the romantically ruined castles, vineyards, glorious abbeys, and scenery of the Danube's Wachau Valley. By dinnertime we'll be checked into our Vienna hotel and ready to experience Paris' eastern rival, the Hapsburg capital—Vienna.

Suggested Schedule	
8:00	Hallstatt (or Salzburg) early departure.
10:00	Tour Mauthausen Concentration Camp.
12:00	Lunch in village of Mauthausen.
13:00	Danube Valley—riverside or autobahn to Melk. Tour town and abbey, drive to Krems and into Wien.
17:00	Arrive Wien, visit tourist information office.
18:00	Check into hotel.
19:00	Stroll through center with A-Z book. Dinner near Am Hof (maybe at Esterhazy Keller), late wine at Brezel Gwolb.
Sleep	Vienna

Transportation
Today is very demanding. Drivers will want the earliest start out from Hallstatt. Follow scenic route 145 through Gmunden to the autobahn and head east. Just after Linz, take the St. Valentine exit. Follow the Mauthausen signs, cross the Donau (Danube), turn left, pass Mauthausen town and follow signs to KZ-lager. From Mauthausen the speedy route is to autobahn to Melk, but if you don't mind the curves and the beauty, follow route 3 along the river.

This region, from Persenbeug to Melk, is Nibelungengau, the 4th and 5th century home of the legendary Nibelung tribe, dramatized in Wagner's opera. Next stop: Melk's great abbey. Cross the bridge and follow the signs not into town but to the "Benediktinerstift," or, abbey (no, Maria wasn't here).

The most scenic stretch of Donau is the Wachau Valley lying between Melk and Krems. From Melk cross the river again and stay on route 3. After Krems route 3 is nearly an autobahn speeding you right into Vienna.

Navigating in Vienna, as in any big European city, is a mess. Study the map and see the series of "ringstrasse" looping out from the Donau. As you approach the city you'll cross the North Bridge and land right on the "gurtel"'—or outer ring. Circle around on this thoroughfare until you reach the "spoke street" you need. Treat the inner ringstrasse the same way.

Train travelers should skip Mauthausen (Dachau outside of Munich has much easier public access) and train straight to Melk where you can tour the abbey and picnic on the scenic Melk-Krems Danube River cruise. Boats (free with Eurailpass) leave Melk at 9:00, 12:30 and 14:30. Call the DDSG boat company's office, 0732/270011 in Linz, or 266536 in Vienna, or the Melk T.I. at 02752/2307 to confirm these times. It's a two-hour ride to the attractive but rather boring town of Krems where you can connect with an hourly 60-minute train ride into Vienna (there's quite a walk from the Krems boat dock to train station). Or, you can stay on board and complete the 5½-hour Melk-Vienna cruise.

If you train directly into Vienna (3½ hours from Salzburg) you can easily do the Wachau train/boat excursion as a day trip later on. Remember the six-knot flow of the Donau makes downstream trips about a third faster.

Sightseeing Highlights—Danube Valley
▲▲▲ **Mauthausen Concentration Camp**—More powerful and less American-oriented than Dachau, this slave labor and death camp functioned from 1938 to 1945 "for the exploitation and extermination of Hitler's opponents." Over half of its 206,000 quarry-working prisoners were killed here. Set in a strangely beautiful setting next to the Danube and its now still and overgrown quarry, Mauthausen is open daily from 8:00-17:00. The camp barracks house a museum (some English labels but it helps to pick up the English booklet) and a graphic movie (top of each hour, German only, but it doesn't really matter). Go downstairs for the most emotionally-moving rooms and gas chamber. The ghosts of the horrors can still be felt. Outside the camp each victim's country has erected a gripping memorial. Many yellowed photos sport fresh flowers. Walk to the barbed wire memorial overlooking the quarry. By touring a concentration camp and putting ourselves through this emotional wringer we are heeding and respecting the fervent wish of the victims of this fascism—that we "never forget." Too many people forget by choosing not to know.
▲▲▲ **Melk Abbey (Benediktinerstift)**—This newly restored abbey beaming proudly over the Danube Valley is one of Europe's great sights. Freshly painted and gilded throughout, it's a Baroque dream, a lily alone. To see its lavish library,

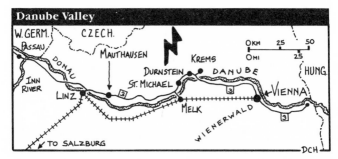

church, palace rooms and the great Danube view from the abbey balcony, you must take a tour. German ones go constantly, English tours only with groups of 20 or more. Open daily 9:00-12:00 and 13:00-17:00, call 02752/2312232 to find out when the next English group is scheduled (normally at 11:30, other times haphazardly). The cute village below makes waiting for a tour pleasant. (Melk T.I. 02752-2307, fine youth hostel tel 2681).

▲▲ **Wachau Valley**—A lovely drive or cruise. Good wine garden and tasting in St Michael for a break. Durnstein is a fly paper luring hordes of tourists with its traffic free quaintness and its one claim to fame—and fortune—Richard the Lion Hearted was imprisoned here in 1193. You can probably sleep in his bedroom.

Vienna Orientation
Vienna is so big and busy and complex that a little chaos would be understandable. Even though administrative districts of the city are called "Bezirks," the place is very orderly and has gone to great lengths to make life easy—if not cheap—for its visitors.

The heart of the city snuggles around the towering St. Stephen's cathedral south of the Donau, held together tightly by the Ringstrasse. This is the first "Bezirk." The "gurtel" is a broader ring road containing the rest of downtown, or Bezirks 2-9. Nearly all our sightseeing will be done in the core first district or along the inner Ringstrasse. As a tourist, concern yourself only with this small old center and the city suddenly becomes manageable.

Vienna's tourist office, located in front of the Opera House under the Ringstrasse, is too small and crowded but excellent. They find rooms and provide visitors with pamphlets on whatever they need. Stop by here first with your sightseeing plan to confirm a list of needs and questions and pick up a city map, list of restaurants, museum hours, walking tour schedule, program of events, Jugendstil flier, transit info and the essential

"Vienna From A to Z" book. This book is really all you need to see the town. Every important building has a flag banner with a number on it that keys into this little guidebook. Every city should spoil its visitors with one of these. Open daily 9:00-19:00, tel 431608, with offices at each train station as well.

Vienna has a fine, though complicated, transit system of buses, trams and subways. To simplify things (even though it probably won't pay for itself) buy the 72-hour pass for 92 AS. I used it mostly to zip along the Ring. Get a transit map with your pass. Without a pass, blocks of 5 tickets at 13 AS each are cheaper than individual rides—18 AS. Don't drive in Vienna. Ask at your hotel where to park your car and leave it there.

Food and Lodging

Vienna, like Munich, has plenty of rooms but nothing cheap. The T.I. room finding service will set you up for a 30 AS charge. Plan to spend $10 for a hostel bed or $35 for a small hotel double. Rooms in a private home are cheap ($10) but three days is the minimum stay and they are far from centrally located. In the summer, call one of these places a few days in advance.

Pension Columbia—Offering classy Old World elegance rare in this price range, friendly Mr. Naschenweng speaks English and will hold a room until 17:00 with a phone call. A great value, 500 AS doubles, 630 triples, 760 quads, with shower. Kochgasse 9, 1080 Wien VIII, tel 426757, tram 5 from West Station, bus 13A from South Station.

Pension Lindenhoff—Lindenhofgasse 4, Vienna 1070, tel 930498. This place is clean and depressing, with good parking, very central location just off Mariahilferstrasse, 12 minutes walk from Hofburg, small breakfast, English spoken, 450 AS doubles.

Esterhazy Pension—Funky and clean but a very depressing entryway—a good example of not judging something by its cover. Also just off Mariahilferstrasse at Nelkengasse 3, Vienna 1060, tel 575159. Trams 52 and 58 take you straight from the Ring. No breakfast, English spoken, 450 AS doubles.

Pension Suzanne—This classy place is just across from the Opera at Walfischgasse 4, tel 5132507. More expensive with 710 AS doubles but nicer too. Call ahead.

International Studenthaus—This is a great value, actually within the Ring, 5 minutes from the Opera, a classy dorm offering 250 AS singles and 350 AS doubles (cheaper with hostel card or for longer stays). Open July 1-Sept 30, 170 beds but often full, call 5128463 between 8:00 and 11:00 to leave name. At Seilerstatte 30, Vienna A-1010.

Porsellaneum der Weiner Universitat—100 AS per person in singles and doubles, open July—Sept, at 9 Porzellangasse 30, between Ring and Franz Joseph Bahnhof, tram D, call 347282 first.

Youth Hostel Neubau—New, cheery, but normally full. B&B for 130 AS, at Myrthengasse 7, tel 936316 or 939429.

The Viennese appreciate the fine points of life, and right up there with sex is eating. The city has many atmospheric restaurants. As you ponder the menus, remember Vienna's diverse empire may be gone but its flavor lingers. You'll find Slavic and Eastern European specialities here along with wonderful desserts and local wine. Three interesting drinks to try are Gruner Veltliner (green wine), Storm (very very new wine, seasonal), and Traubenmost (a heavenly grape juice on the verge of wine, also seasonal, sometimes just called "most").

Here are some restaurants to consider:

Esterhazykeller—Self-service, rowdy, smokey, cheap, easy $4 meals, open 16:00-21:00, at 1 Haarhof near Am Hof, just off Naglergasse.

Augustinerkeller—Fun, like the Esterhazykeller, a bit touristy, two minutes from the Opera under the Albertina Museum at 1 Augustinerstrasse, open from 10:00-23:00.

Rathauskeller—Classy, in the city hall cellar, quite touristy with lots of tour groups, but still a good time and a good value. Live music after 19:00 in the Grinzingerkeller, closed Sundays.

12 Apostles—Most touristy of the "kellers" —skip it.

Zo den 3 Hacken—Great goulash and atmosphere, at 1 Singerstrasse 28. Also check out the restaurant spilling onto the sidewalk one block away on Riemergasse.

Brezel Gwolb—A wonderfully atmospheric wine cellar with outdoor dining on a quiet square as well. Delicious inexpensive light meals, fine krautsuppe, even better for a late glass of wine. 1, Ledererhof 9, off Am Hof.

Zum Scherer Sitz u. Stehbeisl—Untouristy, in or outdoor, soothing woody atmosphere, intriguing decor, local specialties, good wine. At Judenplatz 7, near Am Hof, Mon-Sat 11:00-13:00, Sun 17:00-24:00.

Buffet Trzesniewski—Famous for its elegant and cheap finger sandwiches and small beers. Fun for a light lunch. Just off the Graben, across from Cafe Hawelka, 1 Dorotheergasse, Mon-Fri 9:00-19:30, Sat 9:00-13:00.

Naschmarkt—a cheap and good chain of cafeterias you'll find all over Vienna, $3 meals.

DAY 10

VIENNA

Vienna is a head without a body. Built to rule the once grand
Hapsburg Empire—Europe's largest—she started and lost
WWI, and with it her far flung holdings. Today, you'll find a grand
capital ruling a relatively small and insignificant country.
Culturally, historically, and from a sightseeing point of view, this
city is right up there with Rome, Paris, and London. With 1.6
million people, the town of Freud, Maria Theresa and Strauss
holds 20% of Austria's population. Last night we oriented
ourselves. Today we attack.

Suggested Schedule	
9:00	Ride tram #1 360 degrees around the Ringstrasse, get off at City Hall and walk through Hofburg Gardens to the Opera.
10:30	City orientation tour. Leave it at Belvedere if you want to see 20th century art (Jugendstil).
12:00	Naschmarket, stroll, buy picnic, eat in Berggarten.
13:30	Neuburg museums and Hofburg.
15:00	Kunsthistorisches Museum.
17:00	Tram to Kursalon, Stadtpark. Concert behind Kursalon until 18:00.
19:00	Evening at the Prater amusement park or in old town.
Sleep	Vienna

Sightseeing Highlights
▲▲▲ **Ringstrasse**—In the 1860s Emperor Francis Joseph had
the city's ingrown medieval wall torn down and replaced by a
grand boulevard 190 feet wide arcing 2½ miles around the city's
core. One of Europe's great streets, it's lined with diverse and
interesting architecture. Tram 1 circles the whole route and so
should you.
▲▲ **St Stephan's Cathedral**—Stephansdom is the Gothic
needle that the whole city spins around. With hundreds of
years of history carved in its walls and buried in its crypt (open
10:00-11:30, 14:00-16:30), this is a fascinating starting point
for a city walk. Tours of the church are German only, the 50-
minute daily mass is impressive, the crowded lift to the north
tower (daily 9:00-17:30) shows you a big bell but a bad view.

If you climb the 343 tightly wound steps of the spiral staircase to the watchman's lookout, 246 feet above the postcard stand, you'll be amply rewarded with Vienna's best view. From the top, orient yourself in the town, use your A-Z book to locate the famous sights (open daily 9:00-17:00, March-Nov 15). The church is nearly always open. The Stephansplatz around the square and the nearby Graben ("ditch") street are colorful and lively.

▲▲▲ **Hofburg**—The complex, confusing, and imposing Imperial Palace demands your attention. Home of the Hapsburg emperors until 1918 and still home of the Spanish Riding School, the Vienna Boys' Choir, the Austrian president's office and several important museums. Your A-Z sorts out this time-blackened, jewel-stained mess nicely. While you could lose yourself in its myriad halls and courtyards, after a strolling overview I'd limit your attention to three things:

The Imperial Apartments—These lavish Versailles-type rooms are the ultimate in wish-I-were-God royal interiors. Open Mon-Sat 8:30-16:00, Sun 8:30-12:30, entrance from courtyard under dome of St Michael's Gate. Must be seen with a tour and tours are technically German only. Be sure that every eager wide-eyed English-speaker in your group politely lets your guide know you're dying to hear some English. This is a small downtown version of the even grander Schonbrunn Palace. If you're rushed, skip one or the other.

Treasury—The Weltliche and Geistliche Schatzkammer (secular and religious treasure room) is one of the world's great collections of historical jewels. Don't miss the 1000-year-old crown of the Holy Roman Emperor.

The Neuburg, or new palace, is the last and most impressive addition to the palace (from this century)—and newly opened to visitors. Its grand facade arches around Heldenplatz. Check it out quickly, not only to see its fine collection of weapons, musical instruments, and classical statuary from ancient Ephesus, but to wander among those royal halls, stairways, and painted ceilings. Open Mon, Wed, Thurs and Fri 10:00-16:00, Sat and Sun 9:00-16:00, closed Tuesday.

▲▲ **Opera**—The Staatsoper facing the Ring, just up from Stephansdom and next to the T.I., is a central point for any visitor. While the critical reception of the building 120 years ago led the architect to commit suicide and it's been rebuilt since the WWII bombings, it is a dazzling place and deserves a look. Tours only, daily in English July and Aug at 10:00, 11:00, 13:00, 14:00, 15:00, other months, afternoons only, 25 AS. The Vienna State Opera, with the Vienna Philharmonic Orchestra in the pit is one of the top three opera houses in the world. There are performances almost nightly, except in July and August, with shows normally sold out.

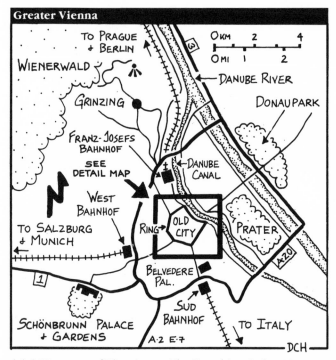

Greater Vienna

TO PRAGUE + BERLIN
WIENERWALD
GRINZING
FRANZ-JOSEFS BAHNHOF
SEE DETAIL MAP
WEST BAHNHOF
TO SALZBURG + MUNICH
RING
OLD CITY
DANUBE RIVER
DONAUPARK
DANUBE CANAL
PRATER
BELVEDERE PAL.
SUD BAHNHOF
TO ITALY
SCHÖNBRUNN PALACE + GARDENS
A·2 E·7
DCH
0 KM   2   4
0 MI 1   2

▲▲▲ **Museum of Fine Arts**—The Kunsthistorisches Museum is the most exciting and varied collection of paintings on our tour. Aside from a fine collection of Egyptian and Classical art, and applied arts including a divine golden salt shaker by Cellini, you'll see the great Hapsburg Collection of masterpieces by the likes of Durer, Rubens, Titian, Raphael, and especially Brueghel. There are no tours or reasonable guidebooks but the paintings are laid out on one easy floor and clear charts are posted to keep you on course. Open Tues-Fri 10:00-18:00, Sat and Sun 9:00-18:00, closed Monday. Picnic in the lovely park outside.

▲▲ **Academy of Fine Arts**—Just three minutes from the Opera, this small but exciting collection includes works by Bosch, Botticelli, Rubens, a Venice series by Guardi, and a self-portrait by 15-year-old Van Dyck. Schillerplatz 3, Tues, Thurs, Fri 10:00-14:00, Wed 10:00-13:00, 15:00-18:00, Sat and Sun 9:00-13:00, 15 AS.

▲ **Albertina Collection of Graphic Arts**—Two minutes from the Opera, this is a lovely collection of sketches by all the masters. For a behind-the-scenes appreciation of Raphael, Durer, or Rubens, study their sketches. I was a bit disillusioned when I learned that the originals are stored away and mostly copies are on display—but it's still worthwhile. Augustinerstrasse 1, open Mon, Tues, and Thurs 10:00-16:00, Wed 10:00-18:00, Fri 10:00-14:00, Sat and Sun 10:00-13:00, closed Sundays in July and August. Rustic, fast and cheap cellar restaurant downstairs.

▲ **Belvedere Palace**—The elegant palace of Prince Eugene of Savoy (conquerer of the Turks) houses the "Austrian Gallery of 19th and 20th century art." Skip the lower palace and focus on the top floor of the upper palace (Oberes Belvedere) for a winning view of the city and a fine collection of Jugendstil art—Klimt and Kokoschka. Fine garden. Tues-Sun 10:00-16:00, entrance at Prince Eugene Strasse 27.

▲▲▲ **Schonbrunn Palace**—The Schloss Schonbrunn is Vienna's finest palace, is second only to Versailles in all of Europe. Located far from the center, it was the Hapsburg's summer residence. It's big—1441 rooms—but only 45 rooms are shown to the public. English tours leave daily at 9:00, 10:00, 11:00, 12:00, 13:30, 14:30, 15:30 and 16:30. Sat and Sun are most crowded; the 15:30 and 16:30 tours are least crowded. Entry includes the required tour and is 50 AS, 10 AS with student card. The 30 AS guidebook gives an unnecessary room by room description but is a nice souvenir. Pass any waiting time around the corner in the four light and happy Bergyl rooms—painted gaily for Maria Theresa by Bergyl (15 AS including an interesting palace history exhibit). The sculpted gardens and Gloriette Park are open til dusk, free, long walk to Gloriette for nothing but a fine city view.

▲▲ **Jugendstil**—Vienna gave birth to its own wonderful brand of Art Nouveau around the turn of the century. It's becoming the rage around Europe, and many come to Vienna solely in search of Jugendstil. There are now city Judendstil walking tours (info at T.I.) and the T.I. puts out a fine Jugendstil brochure. The best of Vienna's scattered Jugendstil sights are in the Belvedere collection, the Karlsplatz subway stop and the Clock on Hoher Markt. The Museum of Applied Arts is disappointing.

▲ **City Park**—Vienna's Stadtpark is a gemutlichkeit world of gardens, memorials to local musicians, ponds, peacocks, music in bandstands, and local people escaping the city. Notice the Jugendstil entry at the Stadtpark subway station. The Kursalon orchestra plays the Strauss waltzes daily from 16:00 to 18:00 and from 20:00 to 22:00. You can buy an expensive ($3 and up) cup of coffee for a front row seat or join the local senior citizens and ants on the grass for a free fringe view.

▲ **Prater**—Vienna's sprawling amusement park tempts any visitor with its huge (220-foot high), famous, but boring ferris wheel (Riesnrad), endless fun food places and rides like the rollercoaster, bumper cars, and Lilliputian Railroad. This is a fun

goofy place to share the evening with thousands of Viennese.
For a family, local-style dinner eat at Wieselburger Bierinsel.
▲ **Nasch Market**—A typical old Vienna produce market
bustles daily, just out from the Opera along Wienzeile Street.
It's a bit seedy, surrounded by sausage stands, cafes, and
theaters, and each Saturday it sprouts a huge flea market.
▲▲ **City Tours**—Of Vienna's many tours, I'd recommend the
"Getting Acquainted" tour that leaves daily from the Opera
at 10:30, 11:45, 15:00 and, in the summer, 16:30. This 75-minute
intro to the city covers a surprising amount of ground for 150
AS. No reservations necessary, tel 7246830. Cut out of the tour
at the Upper Belvedere if you'd like to see the art.
Sunbathing—The Austrians, like most Europeans, worship the
sun. Their lavish swimming centers are as much for tanning
as for swimming. The Krapfenwaldbad is renown as the gathering point for the best looking topless locals.
▲▲ **Music**—Vienna is Europe's music capital but, sadly, in July
and August the biggies are silent. The music season thrives
from October to June reaching a symphonic climax during the
Vienna Festival each May and June. Normally, the bigger halls
attract the best talent. Even in the summer you'll find lots of top
notch classical music. Try to take in a concert somewhere. The
T.I. has ticket info.
▲ **Wine Gardens**—The "Heurigen" is a uniquely Viennese in-
stitution celebrating (and drinking) the "Heuriger," or new
wine. Heurigen restaurants cluster at the edge of town doing
their best to maintain their old village atmosphere and serve
their homemade new wine with light meals and a fun strolling
musicians type atmosphere. There are many Heurigen suburbs.
Grinzing is the most famous and touristy. For a complete listing pick up the T.I.'s brochure. Newstift am Walde (bus 35A) is a
local favorite with much of its original charm intact. (Try Haus
Zimmermanns at Mitterwurzgasse 20, tel 441207). Many locals
say it takes several years of practice to distinguish between
Heuriger and vinegar.
▲▲ **The Viennese Coffee House**—The Viennese living room
is down the street in a cozy coffee house. This tradition is just
another example of the Viennese interest in good living. Vienna's many long-established (and sometimes even legendary)
coffee houses, each with an individual character, offer newspapers, great pastries, sofas, elegance, and a take-all-the-time-
you-want-brother charm for the price of a cup of coffee. The
coffee is very good and very strong. You may want to order
"brauner" (with a little milk) rather than "Schwarzer" (black).
Some of my favorites are: Cafe Hawelka (1, Dorotheergasse 6,
closed Tuesday, just off the Graben) with a wonderful old
"brooding Trotsky" atmosphere, paintings on the walls by

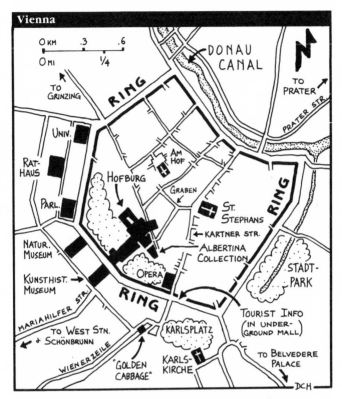

struggling artists who couldn't pay, a saloon wood flavor, chalkboard menu, smoked velvet couches, international selection of newspapers, and a phone that rings for regulars; the Central (1, Herrengasse 14, Jugendstil decor, great topfen strudle); the Sperl (6, Gumpendorfer 11, Jugendstil); and Cafe Ritter (6, Mariahilferstrasse 73, near recommended Esterhazy Pension) true, basic, stylish and interesting local crowd, no tourists, and the best smelling urinals in Europe.

Honorable Mention—Several museums that try very hard but are submerged in the greatness of Vienna are: Historical Museum of the City of Vienna (Karlsplatz); Folkloric Museum of Austria (Laudongasse 15, 8th district); and the Museum of Military History (Heeresgeschichtliches, at 3, Arsenal, Objekt 18) probably Europe's best if you're into swords and shields.

Dishonorable Mention—Considering the very tough competition and your limited sightseeing time, you need to be selective. Be sure to miss these overrated sights: Spanish Riding

School Practice Session (in summer it's the closest you'll get to the famous Royal Lipizzaner stallions, crowded and boring); the homes of Freud, Beethoven, Haydn, Mozart, etc. (Many famous people chose to live in Vienna—unless you're a devotee, skip their houses); City Hall tours (the exterior is lovely, the interior blah); Museum of Applied Arts (disappointing garage sale of Jugendstil furniture); Demels Cafe (with a slow and steady flow of gawking Americans who only miss TV's "Lifestyles of the Rich and Famous" when they're out of the country); and the giant ferris wheel. Sorry, I'm paid to have opinions.

Helpful Hints
The middle two digits of Vienna postal codes designate is the district, or Bezirk. City telephone code is 0222. There is a whole series of city walking tours—pick up the listing at the T.I. You can buy a special coupon booklet good for a 30% discount at all participating national museums.

DAY 11

VIENNA TO THE TYROL

After some last minute sightseeing and some scurry time in
Vienna we'll spend the early afternoon touring the magnificent
Schonbrunn Palace and hit the autobahn for a non-stop 5-hour
drive westward to the Tyrol. We'll spend the night in a small
town just outside Innsbruck before carrying on into Switzerland
tomorrow.

Suggested Schedule	
9:00	Morning free, check out of hotel, possible other museums or browse downtown, St. Stephans.
11:00	Opera tour.
12:00	Lunch at Augustiner Keller or picnic at Schonbrunn.
13:00	Drive to Schonbrunn, tour.
15:00	Hit the autobahn, 5 hour drive to near Innsbruck.
21:00	Arrive, Hall in Tyrol.
Sleep	Hall

Transportation

To leave Vienna, drive along the Gurtel to the West Bahnhof,
turn right and follow the signs to Schloss Schonbrunn which is
directly on the way to the West A-1 autobahn to Linz. There's
plenty of parking at the palace. Leave by 15:00, beating rush
hour, following the autobahn signs to West A-1, passing Linz
and Salzburg, nipping through Germany, turning right onto 93
in the direction of Kufstein and Austria at the Dreieck Inntal.
Crossing back into Austria, you'll follow the scenic (but it'll be
dark) Inn River Valley, stopping 6 miles east of Innsbruck at Hall
in Tyrol. This 5-hour ride is non-stop autobahn all the way.

Eurailers should enjoy the rest of today in Vienna and catch
the overnight train straight to Switzerland. There is a nightly
21:00 departure getting into Zurich at 8:30. Reserve a bed or
couchette at the station when you arrive in Vienna.

Food and Lodging

The problem with today's plan is we arrive late in a popular little
town. Ideally, call in a reservation. Halls' T.I. is open 9:00-12:00
and 14:00-18:00, Sat til 12:00, closed Sunday, tel 05223/6269.
They can find you a room from a long list of zimmers, pensions,
and gasthauses.

Gasthof Badl—This comfortable, friendly, big place run by
the Steiner family is very easy—immediately off the freeway
you'll see its lit sign (noise is no problem). At 350 AS for a small
double it's not cheap but take it for the convenience, the big
breakfast, and the fact that they'll hold a room for a phone call.
Innbruck 4, A-6060, Hall in Tyrol, tel 05223/6784.

Since autobahn reststop food isn't great and you'll probably
be short on time, consider a rolling picnic dinner for tonight. If
you wait till you arrive in Hall the kitchens may be closed.

DAY 12
TYROL TO SWITZERLAND'S APPENZELL

After an easy morning in the town of Hall, a Tyrol mountain joy ride or a look at Innsbruck, we'll picnic at Innsbruck's Olympic ski jump and autobahn for three Alpine hours to Switzerland's moo-mellow storybook friendly Appenzell to bask in the warm, intimate side of the land of staggering icy Alps.

Suggested Schedule	
8:00	Walk through Hall.
9:00	Drive into Innsbruck, see center, tour museum, or skip Innsbruck and joyride) visit Olympic ski jump, picnic there.
12:00	Drive to Switzerland.
15:00	Altstatten, Gais, Stoss (viewpoint).
16:00	Set up in Appenzell, quick visit to Urnasch museum.
20:00	Appenzeller folk evening?
Sleep	Appenzell

SWITZERLAND
16,000 square miles (one-fourth the size of Washington State).
6½ million people (400 per square mile, declining slightly).
One Swiss Franc = 65 cents, 1.6 SF = $1

Switzerland, Europe's richest, best-organized and most mountainous country, is an easy oasis and a breath of fresh Alpine air. Not unlike the Boy Scouts, the Swiss count cleanliness, neatness, punctuality, tolerance, independence, thrift and hard work as virtues. They love the awesome nature that surrounds them and are proud of their many achievements. The average Swiss income (second highest in the world), a great social security system and their super-strong currency, not to mention the Alps, give them plenty to be thankful for.

Switzerland, 60 percent of which is rugged Alps, has distinct cultural regions and customs. Two thirds of the people speak German, 20 percent French, 10 percent Italian, and a small group of people in the southeast speak Romansh, a direct descendant of ancient Latin. Within these four language groups, there are many dialects. An interest in these regional distinctions will win the hearts of locals you meet. As you travel from one valley to the next, notice changes in architecture and

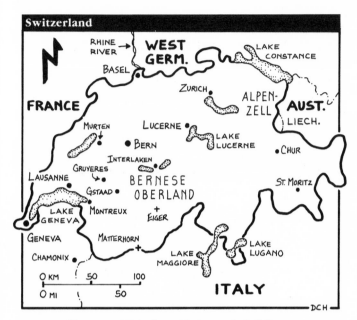

Switzerland

customs (the green Michelin guide is very helpful).

Historically, Switzerland is one of the oldest democracies. Born when three states, or cantons, united in 1291, the Confederation Helvetica as it was called (Roman name for the Swiss—notice "CH" on cars) grew, as our original 13 colonies did, to the 23 of today. The government is very decentralized and the canton is first on the Swiss citizen's list of loyalties.

Switzerland loves its neutrality, stayed out of both world wars, but is far from lax defensively. Every fit man serves in the army and stays in the reserve. Each house has a gun and a bomb shelter. Airstrips hide inside mountains behind Batmobile doors. With the push of a button, all road, rail and bridge entries to the country can be destroyed, changing Switzerland into a formidable mountain fortress. The USSR views Switzerland as a sort of "Capitalist Alamo" and considers its "armed neutrality" charming nonsense. August 1 is the very festive Swiss national holiday.

Switzerland has a low inflation rate and a very strong franc. Accommodations, gas and groceries are reasonable, and hiking is free, but Alpine lifts and souvenirs are expensive. Shops throughout the land thrill tourists with carved, woven and clanging mountain knick-knacks, clocks, watches, and Swiss army knives (Victorinox is the best brand).

The Swiss eat when we do and enjoy rather straightforward, no-nonsense cuisine: delicious fondue, rich chocolates, raclette, fresh dairy products (try Muesli yogurt), 100 varieties of cheese and Fendant, a surprisingly good local white wine. The Co-op and Migros grocery stores are the hungry hiker's best budget bet.

You can get anywhere quickly on Switzerland's fine road system (the world's most expensive to build per mile), or on its scenic and efficient trains. Tourist information offices abound. While Switzerland's booming big cities are quite cosmopolitan, the traditional culture lives on in the Alpine villages. Spend most of your time getting high in the Alps. On Sundays you're most likely to enjoy traditional sports, music, clothing and culture.

Transportation

This morning, after a walk through Hall, you have two choices: a Tyrolean joyride or a look at Innsbruck. If it's sunny, I'd joyride. Backtrack on the freeway to Rattenberg (exit: Kramsach) and take the small riverside road 171 along the Inns through the cute towns of Rattenberg, Schwaz, and Volders. If you'd prefer mountain villages rather than a river valley, cross under the freeway from Hall and climb the scenic road through Tulfes, Rinn, Sistrans and Igls—great scenery. . . great names.

Just south of Innsbruck is the Olympic ski jump (signs say "Bergisel"). Park here and climb to the empty grassy stands for a panoramic picnic before heading west on the autobahn to Landeck and Arlberg. The 8-mile long Arlberg tunnel saves you time but costs $10 and lots of scenery. For a joyride, skip the tunnel, exiting at St Anton, and lose 45 minutes going via Stuben.

For the rainy day city option to the joy ride, autobahn from Hall to the "Innsbruck Ost" exit and follow the signs to the "stadtmitte" or "centrum" and park as close to the old center on the river as you can. There are city buses from Hall that'll get you there stress-free in 30 minutes.

After the Arlberg tunnel, you're just a few minutes from Switzerland. Leave the autobahn just after Feldkirch at Rankweil, taking the small road through Meiningen to Oberriet. As you cross the baby Rhine river, you leave Austria. From there it's an easy scenic drive following the signs through Altstatten and Gais to Appenzell.

By train, I'd streamline things by overnighting it from Vienna to Luzern, spending the morning there, the afternoon in Ballenberg, and getting into the Interlaken region for dinner. Swiss trains are great and you'll have plenty of English-speaking help at each station.

Sightseeing Highlights

▲ **Hall in Tyrol**—Take a lovely "gee, it's great to be alive" walk through this easy-going town. From Gasthof Badl, walk over the old pedestrian bridge into town. The first old building you'll see is the Hasegg castle. Pick up a map and a list of town sights here. Hall has a very colorful morning scene before the daily tour buses arrive. The T.I. offers a daily 10:00 walking tour for 40 AS (in German unless several English-speakers are in the group). They can give you Innsbruck driving instructions and info as well.

▲▲ **Innsbruck**—After Salzburg and Vienna, Innsbruck isn't much. If you do stop, the Golden Roof is the historic center of town. From this square you'll see a tourist information booth with maps and lists of sights, the newly restored Baroque-style Helblinghaus, the city tower (climb it for a great view) and the new Olympics museum with exciting action videos for winter sports lovers.

Nearby are the palace (Hofburg) and church and the very important Tyroler Volkskunst Museum. This museum ($1 open 9:00-17:00 daily, closed Sunday afternoons) is the best look anywhere at traditional Tyrolean lifestyles, with fascinating exhibits ranging from wedding dresses and babies' cribs to nativity scenes. Use the helpful English guidebook ($2).

A very popular mountain sports center and home of the 1964 and 1976 Winter Olympics, Innsbruck is surrounded by 150 mountain lifts, 1,250 miles of trails and 250 hikers' huts. If it's sunny, consider taking the lift right out of the city to the mountaintops above.

▲▲ **Sidetrip over Brennerpass into Italy?**—A short swing into Italy is fast, easy and would give your trip an exciting new twist (easy border crossing, no problem with car, Austrian shillings accepted in the border region). To get there take the great Europa Bridge over Brennerpass. It's expensive (about $8) but in 30 minutes you'll be at the border. In Italy drive to the colorful market town of Vipiteno Sterzing. Just south of town, down a small road next to the autobahn is the Reifenstein Castle. The lady who lives there takes groups through on the hour (with a break from 12:00-14:00) speaking German, Italian and un poco English. It's a unique and wonderfully preserved medieval castle. Tel 0472/65879.

▲ **Vorarlberg**—This westernmost corner of Austria has a special style and charm. Both Feldkirch and Bregenz have well preserved old quarters. For a great one hour walk, drive four miles out of Dornbirn past Gutle to the Rappenlochschlucht gorge (hike from the car park up to a peaceful lake and back through the impressive river gorge).

Side Trip Through Liechtenstein?—If you must see the tiny country of Liechtenstein take this 30-minute detour: Feldkirch south on E77, drive through Schaan and Vaduz, the capital, cross the Rhine at Rotenboden and immediately get on the autobahn heading north from Sevelen to Oberriet.

▲▲▲ **Sightseeing in Appenzell**—Appenzell is Switzerland's most traditional region—and the butt of much local humor because of it. This is "Landsgemeinde" country, where, until recently, entire villages would meet in town squares to vote. And vote meant men only. Even today, there are a few areas left where women can't vote on local issues. A gentle beauty blankets the region overlooked by the 8,200-foot high peak, Santis. As you drive, you'll enjoy an ever-changing parade of finely carved chalets, traditional villages, and photogenic cows.

If you're here between Aug 15 and Sept 15 there's a good chance you'll get in on—or at least have your road blocked by— the ceremonial procession of flower-decked cows and whistling herders in traditional, formal outfits. The festive march down from the high pastures is a spontaneous move by the herding families, and when they finally do burst into town (a slow motion Pamplona) everyone becomes a child, dropping every-thing and running into the streets.

After changing money in picturesque Altstatten, you'll wind up a steep mountain pass. Park at the summit where you see the tiny Stoss railroad station. Cross to the chapel, walk through the meadow, open the electric wire gate and walk past the mellow munching cows to the monument which celebrates a local Appenzeller victory over Hapsburg Austria. From this spectacular spot you can see the Rhine Valley, Liechtenstein, and the moun-tains of Vorarlberg back in Austria. This is an appropriate first stop in fiercely independent Switzerland. Enjoy the sun and the wind, stretch out on the stone for a snooze. This is a perfect picnic spot. Back by the chapel, the Wirtschaftz Stoss Inn is a rustic place for a drink or snack.

Now carry on through Gais and into Appenzell town. This is the most "typical" town around and the best headquarters for the night. The T.I. is very good (8:00-12:00, 14:00-19:00, Sat 9:00-12:00, 14:00-16:00, closed Sun, tel 071-874111, on the main street, Hauptgasse 19). Ask about an Appenzeller folk evening. (Every night somewhere in town, about $3 without dinner). Do your best to see one of these shows tonight. The lit-tle folk museum across the street is very good—unless you're going to its Urnasch equivalent.

Lodging

Switzerland is more expensive than Austria and any time you
get a double for less than $35 you're doing great. But it is
also wonderfully organized—the phone system is easy, great
T.I.s, English spoken regularly, and plenty of excellent youth
hostels and dorm-type alternatives to expensive hotels. If your
budget is tight be sure to chase down youth hostels (many
with "family rooms"—doubles) and keep your eyes peeled for
matrazenlagers ("lager" means dorm).

In Appenzell town the **Gasthaus Hof** offers by far the best
cheap beds in town in its brand new matrazenlager. Dorm beds
cost 10 SF, sheets 4 F, breakfast 4.50 SF. Telephone in advance
071/872210, it's centrally located just off the Landsgemeindeplatz.
The T.I. can set you up in zimmers for 20 SF per person with
breakfast. The private homes at Sonnhalde (tel 873929) and
Sonnenhalbstrasse 14 (tel 871765) are both good.

DAY 13

APPENZELL TO THE BERNER OBERLAND

After a few short stops in cowbell country, we drive four hours
(in Switzerland, "drive" usually means "scenic drive") to the
Interlaken area, spending the afternoon at Switzerland's greatest
open air folk museum, Ballenberg. After climbing through
traditional houses from every corner of this diverse country
and sampling the handicrafts and baking in action, we'll stop
for a look at Interlaken before driving deep into the heart of the
Alps, leaving our car and riding the gondola to the stop just
this side of Heaven—Gimmelwald.

Suggested Schedule	
8:00	Joyride through Appenzell, cheese tour in Stein.
10:00	Drive direct to Ballenberg, picnic enroute.
14:00	Ballenberg museum.
17:00	Quick look at Brienzwiller, drive to Interlaken, 30 minute walk through Interlaken. Drive to Stechelberg for 18:55 lift.
19:00	Walter's Hotel Mittaghorn in Gimmelwald.
Sleep	Gimmelwald

Transportation

Head west out of Appenzell on the Urnasch road taking the first
right (at the edge of town) to Stein. In Stein look for a big
modern building and the Schankaserei sign. From there wind
scenically south to Urnasch and down the small road to Wattwil.
Drive through Ricken, Rapperswil, over the lake, and south-
ward to Brunnen. From Brunnen, one of the busiest, most expensive to build and most impressive roads in Switzerland
wings you along the Urnersee. It's dangerously scenic, so stop
a few times at the many viewpoints to ogle. At Fluelen get on
the autobahn for Luzern, vanishing into a long tunnel. Be careful
to exit at Stans where a small road takes you along the Alpna-
chersee south toward Sarnen. Take the small chunk of
autobahn, continue past Sarnensee to Brienzwiller before
Brienz. A sign at Brienzwiller will direct you to the Ballenberg
Openluft Museum. Park there. From Brienzwiller, drive along
the congested north side of Lake Brienz. Take the blue, not
green, exit sign into Interlaken. Turn right after the bridge and
cruise through the old resort town down its main street past the
cow field a with great Eiger-Jungfrau view on your left and T.I.,
post office, and banks on your right. At the end of town you'll
hit the West Bahnhof. Park there. Allow 30 minutes to drive

from Interlaken to the Stechelberg gondola parking lot. Head south toward Grindelwald and Lauterbrunnen, pass through Lauterbrunnen town, noticing the train station on your left and the funicular across the street on your right, and drive to the head of the valley, a glacier-cut cradle of Swissness, where you'll see the base of the Schilthornbahn (a big gray gondola station). This parking lot is safe and free, ride the 18:55 lift (5 minutes, $3) to Gimmelwald. A steep 100-yard climb brings you to the chalet marked simply "Hotel." This is Walter Mittler's Hotel Mittaghorn. You have arrived.

Eurailers take the Luzern-Brunig-Brienzwiller train. At the Brienzwiller station check your bag, note when later trains depart for Interlaken, buy your Ballenberg ticket, and follow the footpath into the museum. Carry on later by train to Interlaken-Ost. Private trains (not covered by Eurailpass) go from the Interlaken-East station into the Jungfrau region. Ask at the station about discount passes and special fares. Spend some time in Interlaken before buying your ticket to Lauterbrunnen. Take the train to Lauterbrunnen, cross the street to catch the funicular up to Grutschalp where a special scenic train rolls you along the cliff into Murren. From there hike (45 min) downhill or ride the gondola ($3 and a 100-yard uphill backtrack) to Hotel Mittaghorn. If you walk, there's just one road leading out of Murren (marked with good signs for Gimmelwald) and your hotel is the first building you meet in Gimmelwald. Another option is to ride the post bus from Lauterbrunnen to the base of the Stechelberg-Schilthorn gondola and ride up to Gimmelwald from there.

Sightseeing Highlights

Stein— "The Appenzell Showcase Cheese Dairy" (Schankaserei) is open daily from 8:00-14:00, audio-visual presentation and a look at cheese ageing. It's fast, free, and not very important— but they do have cheap boxes of cold iced tea for sale (1 SF). The T.I. and a new folk museum are right next door.

▲ **Urnasch**—An appealing one street town with my nomination for Europe's cutest museum. The Appenzeller Museum (on the town square, open only from 14:00-17:00 daily, July-Oct, Wed, Sat and Sun April-June, closed in winter, 3 SF) brings this region's folk customs to life. Warm and homey, it's a pity it doesn't work into our plan. (Consider a side trip yesterday if you're early enough—it's an easy drive). The Gasthaus Oxchsen, three doors down from the museum, is a fine traditional hotel (64 SF doubles) with good food and wonderful atmosphere. Take a peek at the restaurant. Tel 071/581117.

▲ **Einsiedeln**—Just a few minutes off the road south of Rapperswil is Switzerland's most important pilgrimage church. It's worth a look if you're in the mood—sort of an Alpine Lourdes.

▲▲▲ **Ballenberg**—"The Swiss Open Air Museum Ballenberg" is a rich collection of traditional and historic farmhouses from every region of the country. Each house is carefully furnished and many have a craftsperson working just as people did centuries ago. The sprawling 50-acre park is a natural preserve and provides a wonderful setting for this culture-on-a-lazy-susan look at Switzerland. Don't miss the Thurgau house (#621) which has an interesting wattle and daub display and a fun bread museum upstairs. Use the 2 SF map/guide. The more expensive picture book is a better souvenir than guide. Open daily 9:30-17:30, April 13-Oct 26, 7 SF entry, 2 hour private tours are 45 SF (by prior arrangement), tel 0367/511123, reasonable restaurant inside, and fresh baked or cooked goodies available at several houses. Before leaving, drive through the little wooden village of Brienzwiller, it's a museum itself. Lovely little church.

▲ **Interlaken**—This is the original 19th century Alpine resort when the Romantic movement redefined mountains as something more than cold and troublesome obstacles. In fact, from that time onward, tourists have flocked to the Alps . . ."because they're there." Interlaken's glory days are long gone, its elegant old hotels eclipsed by the new more jet-setty Alpine resorts. It is a good administrative center (good post office with boxes and long distance phone booths, plenty of banks, major trains to all corners of Europe) and shopping town, but I'd give it a once-over quickly and head for the hills. By all means, sleep in the higher villages—not here. T.I., on the main street, open Mon-Fri 8:00-12:00, 13:30-19:00, Sat 8:00-12:00, 13:30-17:00, Sun 16:00-18:00, tel 036/222121. Good info for the whole region. Pick up Bern map, Jungfrau region map, and Jungfrau region timetable.

▲ **Luzern**—Train travelers will probably pass through Luzern. Near the station is the tourist office and the pleasant lakeside old center with its charming covered bridges—well worth a walk. The sightseeing highlight of Luzern is undoubtedly its huge Museum of Transportation (Verkehrshaus des Schweiz) outside of town on the lake (boats and cable cars go there from the center). Europe's best transport museum, it's open daily from 9:00 to 18:00 (Nov-Feb, Mon to Sat 10:00 to 16:00), 10 SF.

Food and Lodging

While Switzerland bustles, Gimmelwald sleeps. It has a youth hostel, a pension, and a hotel. The hostel is simple, less than clean, rowdy, cheap (non-members 12.50 SF, members 5.50 SF), and very friendly. It's often full, so call ahead to Lena, the elderly woman who runs the place (tel 036-551704).

The hostel has a self-serve kitchen and is one block from the lift station. This relaxed hostel is struggling to survive. Please respect its rules, leave it cleaner than you found it, and treat it with loving care. Next door is the pension with rooms and meals. Up the hill is the treasure of Gimmelwald: Walter Mittler, the perfect Swiss gentleman, runs a chalet called **Hotel Mittaghorn**. It's a classic Alpine-style place with a million-dollar view of the Jungfrau Alps. Walter is careful not to get too hectic or big and enjoys sensitive, back door travelers. He runs the hotel alone, keeping it simple but with class. . . He charges about $14 for bed and breakfast. (Address: 3826 Gimmelwald, Bern, Switzerland, tel 036-551658, English spoken.).

Other good budget beds in the region are at **Masenlager Stocki** (Lauterbrunnen, tel 551754), **Naturfreundehaus Alpenhof** (Stechelberg, 551202) and the **Chalet Schweizerheim Garni** ($20 per person in July and Aug, $15 off season, Wengen, 551581). Younger travelers love the cheap and Yankee-oriented **Balmer's Herberge** in Interlaken (Haupstrasse 23, in Matten, tel 036-221961). There are two cheap "lagers" at Kleine Scheidegg (25 SF for B&B, let the Interlaken T.I. telephone them for you) if you want to sleep in the clouds. A great budget bed in Lauterbrunnen is the **Schutzenbach Campground** run by Heinz and Christian von Allmen (most people in this valley are von Allmens). You'll see it on the left just past Lauterbrunnen toward Stechelberg. Open all year, 12 SF/person in 4- to 6-bed rooms, 10 SF in dorms, cheaper off season, must provide your own sheets, self-cooking facilities, tel 036/551268. If you get side-tracked in Brienz, its lakeside hostel (**Strandweg**, tel 036/511152, 10 SF) is great. And for something really different—almost weird—drive up the frighteningly narrow and winding Rosenlaui Valley road south from Meiringen (near Brienz) to the Hilton of the mountain climbers. At 4,000 feet altitude, in the middle of nowhere is the old world tattered but elegant **Berg-Gasthaus Rosenlaui** (50 SF/double, tel 036/712912). At the head of that valley you can hike over Gross Scheidegg and down to Grindelwald. Nearby towns have plenty of budget accommodations. Let each village's tourist office help you out.

For dinner in Gimmelwald, ask Walter when you telephone him earlier, if he's cooking that night. Otherwise there's just the pension in the center of the village. If you're at the hostel, bring some groceries and use the members' kitchen.

DAY 14

FREE DAY IN THE ALPS

Today is your vacation from this go-go vacation. And a great place to recharge your touristic batteries is up here high in the Alps where distant avalanches, cowbells, the fluff of a down comforter, and the crunchy footsteps of happy hikers are the dominant sounds.

If the weather's good we'll ride the lift from Gimmelwald to a classy breakfast at the 10,000-foot Schilthorn's revolving restaurant. Linger among Alpine whitecaps before riding or hiking down to Murren and home to Gimmelwald.

Suggested Schedule

None.   You're on vacation!

Sightseeing Highlights
Evening fun in Gimmelwald is found at the hostel (lots of young Alp-happy hikers and a good chance to share information on the surrounding mountains) and up at Walter's. Walter's bar is a local farmer's hangout. When they've made their hay, they come here to play. They look like what we'd call "hicks" but they speak some English and can be fun to get to know. Walter knows how many beers they've had according to if they're talking, fighting, singing, or sleeping. For less smoke and some powerful solitude, sit outside and watch the sun tuck the mountaintops into bed as the moon rises over the Jungfrau.

Helpful Hints
Walter serves a great breakfast, but if the weather's good, skip his and eat atop the Schilthorn, at 10,000 feet, in a slowly revolving mountain-capping restaurant (of James Bond movie fame). The early-bird special gondola tickets (rides before 9:00) take you from Gimmelwald to the Schilthorn and back with a great continental breakfast on top for about $25. (Get tickets at the Station or from Walter). Try the Birchermuesli-yogurt treat.

For hikers: The gondola ride (Gimmelwald-Schilthorn-Gimmelwald) costs about $25. The hike (G-S-G) is free, if you don't mind a 5,000-foot altitude gain. I ride up and hike down or, for a less scary hike, go up and halfway down by cable car, then walk down from the Birg station. Lifts go twice an hour and the ride takes 30 minutes. (The round-trip excursion early-bird fare is cheaper than Gimmelwald-Schilthorn-Birg. If you

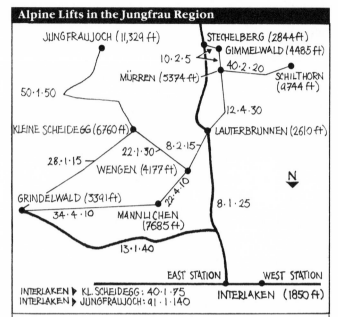

Alpine Lifts in the Jungfrau Region

JUNGFRAUJOCH (11,329 ft)

STECHELBERG (2844ft)

GIMMELWALD (4485 ft)

10·2·5

MÜRREN (5374 ft)

40·2·20

SCHILTHORN (9744 ft)

50·1·50

12·4·30

KLEINE SCHEIDEGG (6760 ft)

LAUTERBRUNNEN (2610 ft)

22·1·30

8·2·15

28·1·15

WENGEN (4177 ft)

N

GRINDELWALD (3391ft)

22·4·10

34·4·10

MANNLICHEN (7685 ft)

8·1·25

13·1·40

EAST STATION

WEST STATION

INTERLAKEN ▶ KL. SCHEIDEGG : 40·1·75
INTERLAKEN ▶ JUNGFRAUJOCH : 91·1·140

INTERLAKEN (1850 ft)

Code: Roundtrip price in Swiss francs—Departures per hour—Length of ride in minutes (e.g., 13-1-40 is 13 SF roundtrip, 1 per hour, 40 minutes long).

Round trips are discounted only above towns (i.e., to Kl. Scheidegg & Schilthorn). Buy one-way between towns for flexibility. Maps, schedules and price lists are available at any station. Lifts run from about 7 am to 8 pm. Groups of five or more receive about a 20% discount. Discount Jungfraujoch trains leave Kl. Scheidegg at 8:07, 9:07, 15:03, 16:00 and 17:10. Other rides cost 16 SF more than price above. Stechelberg to Gimmelwald: 25 & 55 past the hour, until 19:25.

buy the ticket you can decide at Birg if you want to hike or ride down). Linger on top. Watch hang gliders set up, psych up and take off, flying 30 or 40 minutes with the birds to distant Interlaken. Walk along the ridge out back. You can even convince yourself you climbed to that perch and feel pretty rugged. Think twice before descending from the Schilthorn (weather can change, have good shoes). Most people would have more fun hiking down from Birg. Just below Birg is a mountain hut. Drop in for soup, cocoa, or a coffee-schnapps. You can spend the night for $5, tel 036/552640.

The most interesting trail from Murren to Gimmelwald is the high one via Gimmlin. Murren has plenty of shops, bakeries, tourist information, banks, and a modern sports complex for rainy days.

Ask at the Schilthorn station for a souvenir pin or sticker. Gimmelwald is so undeveloped because it's classified "avalanche zone." It's one of the poorest places in Switzerland and many of the farmers, unable to make it in their disadvantaged trade, are subsidized by the government. Be careful not to confuse obscure Gimmelwald with very touristy and commercialized Grindelwald just over the Kleine Scheidegg ridge.

DAY 15

BERNER OBERLAND HIKE TO LAKE GENEVA

This morning we'll enjoy the region's most exciting hike, making a loop up from Lauterbrunnen through Mannlichen, Kleine Scheidegg and Wengen. After lunch it's south into French-speaking Switzerland. With plenty of mountain beauty along the way we'll end the day in an entirely different mode touring the romantic Chateau Chillon on the edge of Lake Geneva.

Suggested Schedule	
7:30	Breakfast.
8:00	Lift to car, drive to Lauterbrunnen. Lift to Mannlichen (via Wengen), hike down to Wengen.
12:00	Lunch in Wengen, train to car.
13:00	Drive down Simmental, coffee at Taveyanne village.
16:00	Chateau Chillon.
17:00	Check into hotel or YH. Evening stroll along Montreux promenade.
Sleep	Montreux

Transportation
If the weather's good leave Gimmelwald as early as possible. Park at the large multi-storied pay lot behind the Lauterbrunnen station, buy a ticket to Mannlichen and catch the train. Ride past great valley views to Wengen where you'll walk across town (don't waste time here if it's clear) buy a picnic if you like and catch the Mannlichen lift (departing every 15 minutes) to the top of the ridge high above you and spend the morning hiking back down.

From Lauterbrunnen head north catching the autobahn (direction Spiez, Thun, Bern) just before entering Interlaken. After Spiez turn left (direction Zweisimmen) into the Simmental Valley. After Saanen pass through the very rich and "in" resort town of Gstaad (notice all the suits, ties, and poodles—what a vacation!) and over the Col du Pillon pass. From here the most scenic route to Montreux forks left on the Villars road. Once you hit the Rhone Valley take the small road, not the autobahn, to Lac Leman (Lake Geneva) and stop at the Chateau Chillon, parking on the road at the castle.

Train travelers will find trains leaving about every hour for the three-hour ride down Simmental to Montreux.

Bernese Oberland

Sightseeing Highlights

▲▲▲ The Mannlichen-Kleine Scheidegg Hike—This is my favorite Alpine hike, entertaining you all the way with glorious Eiger, Monch and Jungfrau views. From the top of the Mannlichen lift hike to the little peak for that "king of the mountain" feeling. Then walk about an hour around to Kleine Scheidegg for a picnic or restaurant lunch. If you've got an extra $40 and the weather's perfect, ride the train through the Eiger to the towering Jungfraujoch and back. From Kleine Scheidegg, enjoy the everchanging Alpine panorama of the North Face of the Eiger, Jungfrau and Monch, probably accompanied by the valley-filling mellow sound of alp horns, as you hike gradually downhill (two hours) to the town of Wengen. If the weather turns bad or you run out of steam, you can catch the train earlier. The trail is very good and the hike is easy for any fit person. Wengen is a fine shopping town. Avoid the steep and boring final descent by catching the train from Wengen to Lauterbrunnen. (To check the weather before investing in a ticket, call 551022.)

▲ Simmental—The Simmen Valley ("tal" means valley) is famous in the USA for its great milk cows. It's known locally for its fine medieval churches (the most in the Berner Oberland)

and for the American farmers who come to see the cows. The Erlenbach church (park at the market square) is worth a look. The English brochure explains that like most local churches, the beautiful paintings decorating the interior were white-washed over in the 16th century.

▲▲ **Glacier des Diablerets**—For another grand Alpine trip to the top of a 10,000-foot peak depart from Reusch or Col du Pillon on the three-part lift. A quick trip takes about 90 minutes and costs 32 SF—you could stay for lunch. From the top, on a clear day, you can see the Matterhorn and even a bit of Mont Blanc, Europe's highest mountain. This is your only good chance to do or watch some summer skiing. Normally expensive and a major headache to accomplish, it isn't bad here. Lift ticket, rental skis, poles, boots and a heavy coat cost 30 SF. Since the slopes close at 14:00, you'd have to drive here direct from Gimmelwald to manage.

▲▲ Taveyanne—One of the most enchanting and remote villages in Switzerland, Taveyanne is 2 miles off the main road between Col de la Croix and Villars. A small sign will point you down a small road on the left. It's just a jumble of log cabins and snoozing cows stranded all alone at 5,000 feet. The only place in town is the **Refuge de Taveyanne** where the Sieben-thal family serves hearty meals (great fondue and a delicious "croute au fromage avec oeuf" for 11.50 SF) in a prize-winning rustic setting—no electricity, low ceilings, huge charred fire-place with a cannibal-sized cauldron, prehistoric cash register, and well-hung ornamental cowbells. This is French Switzerland and these people speak nothing else. For a special experience consider sleeping in their primitive loft—it's never full, 6 mat-tresses, access by a ladder outside, 7 SF, tel 025/681947.

▲▲▲ **Chateau Chillon**—This wonderfully preserved 13th century castle set romantically at the edge of Lac Leman is a joy. Follow the English brochure from one fascinating room to the next—tingly views, a dank prison, weapons, interesting fur-niture and even 700-year-old toilets. The long climb to the top of the keep (#25 in the brochure) isn't worth the time or sweat. Open 9:00-18:00 daily, 4 SF, easy parking.

Food and Lodging

Resorty Lac Leman (Lake Geneva) is expensive. Call ahead, stay inland, or prepare to spend. The perfect answer is the **"Haut Lac" Youth Hostel** in the town of Territet (Passage de l'auberge 8, 1820 Territet). It's situated on the lake, a ten minute stroll north of Chateau Chillon, friendly, no traffic noise, English spoken, members only, any age, closed from 9:00-17:00, will hold a bed till 18:00 if you telephone (021/634934), 14 SF for sheets, bed and breakfast, 10 SF extra if you want the privacy of a double. Dinner at 18:30 for 8 SF.

If you're not a hosteler try **Villa Tilda** (along the lake on Quai Vernex, tel 633814, 8 minutes from the station) or **Pension Wilhelm** (also near the station at Rue du Marche 13, tel 631431). Otherwise, Montreux's T.I. is open till 18:00 and if you telephone 021/631212 they'll tell you how much poorer you'll be by tomorrow morning (cheapest doubles normally 80 SF).

Itinerary Options

Never overestimate the size of Switzerland. With its fine roads you could actually do everything in side-trips from a head-quarters in the Interlaken district. Or you could see Chateau Chillon and drive up to Murten tonight.

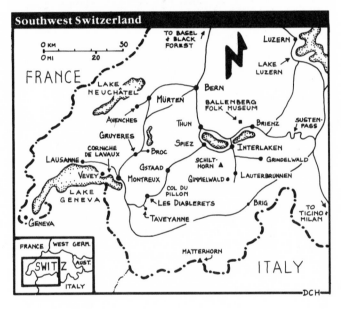

Southwest Switzerland

DAY 16

THE HIGHLIGHTS OF FRENCH SWITZERLAND

After a look at Montreux and the Swiss Route du Vin we'll leave scenic Lac Leman to explore the fragrant home of Gruyeres cheese, tour a chocolate factory, and settle in Switzerland's best-preserved walled town.

Suggested Schedule

8:00	Check out of hotel, browse through Vevey market and waterfront.
9:00	Explore Corniche de Lavaux.
10:00	Drive to Gruyeres district.
11:00	Musee Gruerien in Bulle, buy picnic (both close at noon).
12:15	Picnic at Gruyeres town. Afterwards see cheese demo.
14:00	Tour Caillers Chocolate Fabrique in Broc.
15:30	Drive small road to Murten.
17:00	Set up in Murten (or Avenches YH).
18:00	Explore Murten, ramparts, old town.
Sleep	Murten

Transportation
After driving through Montreux and parking along the water-front for a short stop in Vevey things get a little more complex. We want to continue along the lake past Vevey, not on the waterfront road nor on the parallel autobahn just above it, but along the narrow twisting Corniche de Lavaux for a tour of the Swiss vineyards. From Vevey follow signs to Mondon and Chexbres. When you're ready to leave the lake, get on the autobahn and backtrack nearly to Vevey where the super freeway swoops north and in a short while you're exiting at Bulle. The museum Gruerien is well signposted in the center of Bulle. From there it's a 5-minute drive to Gruyeres.

Just before the "driveway" into Gruyeres you'll see a modern "cheeserie" on the right. Drop in for the demo. Then drive up the little road leading into the fortified traffic-free Gruyeres. Try to park at the second, closer lot. For the chocolate factory in Broc, five minutes away, follow the signs to "Broc Fabrique" to the left just before the town square. If you're running out of film avoid the small road from Broc directly north to Fribourg—

it's lined with picturesque houses and villages. Try to avoid driving in Fribourg (actually if you don't mind traffic, it's a fascinating town to spend a few miles just bungling around in). Signs to Bern will eventually lead you to signs to Murten.

Trains go regularly from Montreux through Lausanne to Fribourg where a tiny line will connect you to Murten.

Sightseeing Highlights
▲ **Lac Leman (Lake Geneva)**—Separating France and Switzerland, surrounded by Alps, and lined with a collage of castles, towns, museums and vineyards, Lac Leman's crowds are understandable.

Boats carry its visitors comfortably to all sights of importance, and Eurailers sail for free. The 11 SF ride from Lausanne to Chillon takes 90 minutes with stops in Vevey and Montreux (departing from Lausanne: 8:50, 10:50, 12:45, 14:00, 14:50, and 18:05, departing from the castle: 9:10, 12:29, 15:36, 16:23 and 17:19). Get the full story from any T.I. on the lake.

Montreux is an expensive resort with a famous jazz festival each July. Vevey nearby is a smaller and more comfortable resort town (Charlie Chaplin's last home). The Corniche de Lavaux is the Swiss Wine Road. Its picturesque towns, rugged winding roads and stingy vineyards attract and impress lots of tourists, producing most of Switzerland's tasty but expensive wine. Hikers can take the boat to Cully and explore on foot from there. Drivers can see it quick and easy from their cars.

The most interesting city on the lake is Lausanne. You can park near its impressive cathedral and walk through the colorful old town. The Collection de l'Art Brut (at 11 Ave des Bergieres, open Tues-Fri 10:00-12:00, 14:00-18:00, Sat and Sun 14:00-18:00) is a fascinating and very thought-provoking collection of art by people who have been labeled criminal or crazy by our society.

The big city of Geneva bores me—sterile, cosmopolitan, expensive and full of executives, diplomats, and tourists looking for profits, peace, and cheap rooms.

▲▲ **Musee Gruerien**—Somehow the unassuming little town of Bulle built a refreshing, cheery, folk museum that teaches you all about life in these parts and leaves you feeling very good. It's small and easy, open Tues-Sat 10:00-12:00, 14:00-17:00, Sun 14:00-17:00, 4 SF and 1 SF for the excellent English guide. When it's over a sign reminds you "The Golden Book of Visitors awaits your signature and comments. Don't you think this museum deserves another visit? Thank you!"

▲▲ **Gruyeres**—This ultra-touristy town fills its fortified little hilltop like a bouquet. Its ramparts are a park and its ancient buildings serve the tourist crowds. The castle is mediocre and you don't need to stay long, but make a short stop—it's a wonderful setting. This is the home of Gruyeres cheese and the modern production center in the valley at the foot of the town gives a worthwhile (free and nonstop) look at how the cheese is made. Open 6:00-18:00 daily. Cheese is actually being made from 9:00 to 11:30 and from 13:00 to 15:30. Hotels in town charge a minimum of 80 SF per double.

▲ **Caillers Chocolate Factory**—The nearby town of Broc is dominated by a huge chocolate factory. While you're in Switzerland it's fun to see how all the great chocolate is actually made. This factory gives free one-hour tours with samples March-Oct on Tues, Wed and Thurs from 9:00 to 10:15 and from 13:30 to 15:30. Closed in July. Tel 029/61212 to check. Note: If this factory's hours don't fit yours, we'll be passing the Toblerone factory tomorrow. The Toblerone tour is better but tomorrow is a busier day.

▲▲▲ **Murten**—The finest medieval ramparts in Switzerland surround the 4,600 people of Murten—or "Morat" in French (we're on the lingua-cusp of Switzerland here). The town has three parallel streets, the middle one nicely arcaded, a mediocre castle and city museum, a lovely setting overlooking the tiny Murtensee and the rolling vineyards of gentle Mount Vully in the distance. Try some Vully wine. The only required sightseeing is to do the rampart ramble. The T.I., tel 037/715112, is very friendly and has a handy town walk brochure.

▲ **Avenches**—This quiet little town, a few miles south of Murten, was the capital of Helvetica—Roman Switzerland. Back then its population was 50,000. Today it sleeps with the well-worn ruins of the 15,000 seat Roman amphitheater and an interesting Roman museum.

Food and Lodging

An evening in Murten is so atmospheric that it's worth the splurge. The cheapest doubles in town rent for 60 SF. Try **Hotel Ringmauer** on Deutsche Kirchgasse near the wall on the side farthest from the lake. Frau Gutknecht charges 60 SF per double and runs a pleasant local-style restaurant downstairs (tasty Rosti). Tel 037/711101.

The nearest **hostel** is a beauty—small, clean and laid back—in Avenches at Rue du Lavoir 5, tel 037/752666, 14 SF or 19 SF in a double, open from 7:00-9:00 and from 17:00-22:00 as usual. Call ahead. This is the only budget alternative to a hotel around, unless you want to struggle with Bern tonight and go to its hostel (Weihergasse 4, down the stairs from the parliament building on the river. Open daily 7:00-9:00, 17:00-24:00, lounge open all day, big, efficient, institutional, 8 SF, 15 SF without a card, tel. 031/226316. 30 minute drive from Murten).

DAY 17

BERN TO THE BLACK FOREST

We'll spend most of the day in the Swiss capital city of Bern. Stately but human, classy but fun, this is our best look at urban Switzerland. Then we'll return to Germany, making a small town in the legendary Black Forest home for the night.

Suggested Schedule	
8:30	Drive to Bern.
9:00	Stop at Toblerone factory or go directly to Bern.
10:30	Park at Bern station, T.I. for info.
11:00	Tour Bundeshaus.
12:30	Lunch (consider river swim below Parliament).
14:30	Explore old town, shop arcades, bear pits, view from rose garden.
16:30	Drive to Staufen.
19:00	Check into hotel.
Sleep	Staufen

Transportation
Bern is just 30 autobahn minutes from Murten. If you missed the chocolate at Broc, the impressive new Toblerone factory overlooks the autobahn about five minutes outside Bern. You'll see the factory on the right; take the Bernwohlen exit. As you enter Bern follow signs to "centrum" and "Bahnhof." When you cross the bridge you're near the station. Park in a pay lot near the station where you'll find the T.I. (If you picked up a Bern map in Interlaken, remember to use it). Leaving Bern, follow autobahn signs for Zurich and Basel. Stay on E4 until you get to Basel where Germany and France touch Switzerland.

Before Basel, you'll go through a tunnel and come to Reststatte Pratteln Nord, a strange orange structure that looks like a huge submarine laying eggs on the freeway. Stop here for a look around one of Europe's greatest freeway stops. There's a bakery and grocery store for picnickers, a restaurant and a change desk open daily until 21:00 with rates 2% worse than banks. Spend some time goofing around, then carry on.

At Basel follow the signs to "Deutschland" and then to "Karlsruhe." Once in Germany the autobahn will take you along the French border which for now is the Rhine River. Exit at Bad Krozingen, just before Freiburg, and cut down to Staufen. Park aong the little river and you're just a bridge away from your hotel.

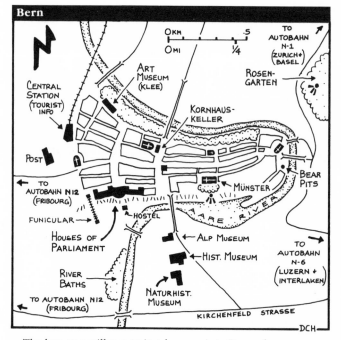

The bus or a milkrun train takes you into Bern where an hourly train takes you to Basel in 75 minutes. Eurailers should homebase in Freiburg (in Germany, not to be confused with the Fribourg in Switzerland) and at least one train per hour makes the 40-minute Basel-Freiburg trip.

Orientation—Bern

If you must spend time in a big Swiss city, there's no doubt Bern's the one. The old town of Switzerland's capital fills a peninsula bounded by the River Aare. The main street (which changes its name several times) cuts the peninsula in half connecting the train station at the top with the popular "bear pits," or "Graben," over the bridge at the bottom. Trolley cars run up and down this axis. (#12 takes you from the pits back to the station.)

For a short well-organized visit: park your car at the station, visit the tourist office inside (open 8:00-20:30 daily, til 18:30 in winter, tel 03/227676, pick up map, list of museums and confirm your plans), follow the intro walking tour on the T.I. city map browsing your way downhill. Finish with a look at the "Graben" and a city view from the Rose Garden and catch a trolley back up to the station.

Sightseeing Highlights

▲▲▲ **Old Town**—Window-shopping and people watching through the lovely arcaded streets and busy market squares is Bern's top attraction. The clock tower (zytgloggeturm) performs at 4 minutes before each hour (tour its medieval mechanics daily at 4:30, tickets 3 SF at T.I. or on the spot). The Munster, or Cathedral, is worth a look. Climb the spiral staircase 100 yards above the town for a great view, good exercise, and a chance to meet a live church watchman. Peter Probst lives way up there watching over the church, answering questions, and charging tourists for the view. Nearby is the imposing Parliament building (Bundeshaus) of Switzerland (free, 45-minute tours most days at 9:00, 10:00, 11:00, 14:00, 15:00 and 16:00, tel 031/618522 to confirm. Closed March, June and Sept, five people minimum group size). Don't miss the view from the Parliament terrace. You may see some national legislators but you wouldn't know it—everything looks very casual.

▲ **Bear Pits** and **Rose Garden**—The symbol of Bern is the bear, and some lively ones frolic their days away to the delight of locals and tourists alike in the big barren concrete pits, or "Graben." Up the street is the Rosengarten. Worth the walk for the great city view.

▲ **The Berner Swim**—For something to write home about, join the local merchants, legislators, publishers, and students in a lunchtime float down the Aare River. The Bernese, proud of their very clean river and their basic ruddiness, have a tradition—sort of a wet, urban paseo—of hiking upstream 15 to 30 minutes and floating playfully or relaxed back down to the excellent (and free) riverside baths and pools (Aarebad) just below the Parliament building. If the river is a bit much, you're welcome to enjoy just the Aarebad.

▲▲ **Museum of Fine Arts (Kunstmuseum)**—Located 4 blocks from the station, it features 1000 years of local art and some Impressionism, but the real hit is its fabulous collection of Paul Klee paintings. If you don't know Klee, I'd love to introduce you. Open Wed-Sun 10:00-17:00, Tues 10:00-21:00.

Other Bern Museums—Across the bridge from the Parliament building on Helvetiaplatz are several museums (Alpine, Berner History, Postal) that sound more interesting than they are. Albert Einstein's House is an interesting stop in the town center on the main street.

▲▲ **Toblerone Chocolate Factory**—The Suchard-Tobler Company has opened a huge new factory and it proudly offers visitors a movie, a mouth-watering English tour through seas of molten chocolate and vats of samples. It's a very impressive place—especially if you like Toblerone. Tours are Tues, Wed and Thurs at 9:00 and 13:30, Mon at 13:30 only, closed July and Oct, tel 031/343511 to confirm plans.

▲ **Staufen in Breisgau**—This is a cute ("cute" is the standard Black Forest adjective) town in the Black Forest. It's a mini-Freiburg—a perfect combination of smallness and off-the-beaten-pathness with a quiet pedestrian zone of colorful old buildings bounded by a happy creek which actually babbles. There's nothing to do here but enjoy the marketplace atmosphere in the morning. Hike through the vineyards to the ruined castle overlooking the town and savor a good dinner with local wine.

Food and Lodging

The Black Forest has lots of hotels and enough visitors to often fill them. It's wise to call ahead. Staufen makes a good overnight stop. The T.I. (Mon-Fri 8:00-16:30, Thurs till 18:00, Sat 9:00-11:00, Sunday closed, tel. 07633/80536) has room lists and can help.

Try to stay at **Hotel Kreuz Post**. It's friendly, immaculate, has lots of character, cute rooms, good food, right in the pedestrian zone just over the bridge. Hauptstrasse 65, 7813 Staufen/Breisgau, tel 07633/5240, closed Wed at 14:00 until Friday morning, 47 DM per double.

Hotel Sonne is also downtown, classier and more expensive, 75 DM per double, tel 97633/7012.

Gasthaus Bahnhof is colorful in a ruddy way. This is the cheapest place in town, across from the very sleepy station, castle out back, no breakfast, self-cooking facilities, a little depressing. 20 DM per person. Tel 07633/6190.

Gasthaus Rossle in the hamlet of St. Ulrich, 15 minutes northeast of Staufen, is my rural choice. In a woodsy typical Schwarzwald setting, with fine beds and great food, a very traditional local-style place, only locals. 24 DM per person, tel 07633/252. Drive on to the end of the road for the view and a walk.

Train travelers may choose to sleep in Freiburg. The T.I., two blocks in front of the station, tel 0761/216, can find you a 60 DM double. The big, modern **hostel** is at the edge of town at Kartauserstrasse 151, tram 1 to Romerhof, tel 0761/67656, 14 DM.

DAY 18

THE BLACK FOREST—SCHWARZWALD

We'll spend the day exploring the best of this most romantic of German forests. By late afternoon we'll be set up in Germany's greatest 19th century spa resort and ready for a stroll through its elegant streets and casino, finishing the day with a "kur"— sauna, massage, and utter restfulness.

Suggested Schedule

8:00	Stroll Staufen.
9:00	Freiburg, park near tourist office. Enjoy pedestrian zone, Munster Platz, Augustina Museum, buy picnic.
11:30	Drive into Black Forest, picnic at or near St. Peter.
14:00	Drive north to Baden-Baden.
15:00	Baden-Baden, get set up, browse through elegant town center.
17:00	Take the kur.
20:00	Dine downtown.
22:00	Stroll Lichtentaler Alley.
Sleep	Baden-Baden

Transportation

From Staufen drive to Freiburg, parking near the T.I. or station (signs "bahnhof"). The center of town is a pedestrian zone circled by a ring road with lots of parking. Leave Freiburg on Schwarzwaldstrasse which becomes scenic #31 down Hallental toward Titisee. Turn left at Hinterzarten onto road 500 turning later to drive through the towns of St. Margen and St. Peter. From St. Peter take the winding Kandelhof road to Waldkirch where a fast road will take you to the "Freiburg Nord" autobahn entrance and you'll autobahn north toward Karlsruhe and Baden-Baden. Follow the autobahn into Baden-Baden. If you're heading for the youth hostel turn left at the first light after the freeway ends, and follow the signs winding uphill to the big modern hostel next to a public swimming pool. Otherwise drive straight into town until you see the T.I. signs near a fountain-filled park.

Train travelers will need to simplify. After probably sleeping in Freiburg let the T.I. recommend the most scenic public transportation route to get to Baden-Baden (hourly 90-minute rides). Consider the Schauinsland excursion and the Freiburg-

Baden-Baden train. The "Baden-Oos" station is 5 miles from
the center. Take bus 1 or 3 to Augustaplatz. (Hostelers get off
long before the center at Grosse Dollen Strasse).

Orientation

The Black Forest, or Schwarzwald, is impressively Catholic and
traditional. On any Sunday you'll find "folks marches," traditional costumes, and a particularly heavy load of local color. It's
a range of hills stretching north-south along the French border
from Karlsruhe to Switzerland. It's so thickly wooded the people called it black. Today it's popular for its clean air, cheery
villages, hiking possibilities and cuckoo clocks.

While many parts are layered with commercialism, our proposed route fills your day with intriguing looks at local life
and lots of Schwarzwald beauty.

Sightseeing Highlights

▲▲ Freiburg—This "sunniest town in Germany" with 180,000
people, 22,000 students, university town vibrancy, French and
Austrian history, bombed and rebuilt since WWII, is the "capital" of the Schwarzwald. It's pleasant, but nothing to telephone
home about. Enjoy its pedestrian-only old center. Freiburg's
trademark is its system of "Bachle" or tiny streams running
down each street. Very fresh and clean today, but imagine back
500 years when these were the town's sewer system. Absorb the
ambience of ice cream and street singers on the cathedral, or
Munster, square. The actual church with a towering tower (not
worth the 116 meter ascent) is impressive. Don't miss the
Augustiner Museum for a fine look at local culture and a great
close-up look at some of the Munster's medieval stained glass
downstairs. (open 10:00-17:00, Wed 10:00-20:00, all of
Freiburg's museums are free).

The T.I. (between old center and station, tel 0761/216) has a
fine 3 DM city guidebook, room-finding service, and info on
the entire Black Forest region. Bounce your plan for the day off
these people. They offer daily guided walks.

▲ Schauinsland—Freiburg's "own mountain" is the handiest
quick look at the Schwarzwald for those carless ones (it was
designed for Freiburgers relying on public transportation). At
its 4,000 foot summit there is a "panorama restaurant," pleasant
circular walks, a tower on a nearby peak offering a commanding
Black Forest view, and the Schniederli—a 1592 farmhouse
museum. Ask at the T.I. for the package rate from Freiburg. 14 DM
will get you there and back including the town center-to-lift
tram ride. The Schauinsland gondola is one of Germany's oldest.

▲ **Badenweiler**—An idyllic but poodle-elegant and finicky-clean spa town known only to the wealthy Germans who soak there; if ever a town was a park, Badenweiler is it. Next to the ruins of a Roman mineral bath in a park of imported and exotic trees (including a California redwood) is the Markgrafen-bad (bath). This prize-winning piece of architecture perfectly mixes the trees and peace with a elegant indoor-outdoor swimming pool. It's open to the public (Mon, Wed, Fri 8:00-20:00, Tues, Thurs and Sat 8:00-18:00, Sun 9:00-18:00, 9 DM). The locker procedure is quite different and the language barrier may nearly sink you. Towels, caps and suits rentable. For a sauna: men—Mon 17:00-21:00, women—Wed 17:00-21:00, mixed sauna (nude) on Fridays 17:00-21:00, 10 DM. My wife and I happened in on a Friday evening and had no choice but to get comfort-able with a handful of naked German strangers and one French-man who comes over every week. "Travel as a temporary Euro-pean" is what I always say!

▲▲ **The Scenic Black Forest Drive**—This pleasant loop from Freiburg takes you through the most representative chunk of the area, avoiding the touristy and over-crowded Titisee. Stop whenever you can to enjoy the clean "healthy" air that doctors actually prescribe for people from all over Germany. A fine hiking center is the town of St. Peter. Its T.I., just next to the fine church, open Mon-Fri 7:30-12:00, 13:30-17:00, can recommend a walk. Without any long stops, this route will get you from Freiburg to Baden-Baden in three hours.

▲▲▲ **Baden-Baden**—Of all the high class resort towns I've seen, Baden-Baden is the easiest to enjoy on a budget in blue-jeans. 150 years ago this was *the* playground of Europe's elite with the world's top casino. Royalty and aristocracy would come from all corners to "take the kur"—soak in the curative (or at least they feel that way) mineral waters. Today this town of 50,000 attracts a more middle class crowd and serves as a great homebase for northern Black Forest explorations.

Baden-Baden has a tremendous tourist office complete with lounge and library (right in the center near the riverside park at Augustaplatz 8, Mon-Sat 9:00-22:00, Sun 10:00-22:00, tel 07221-275200).

The best approach to Baden-Baden, given our tight schedule, is to get set up by 16:00 and spend one hour just browsing through the center, enjoying ritzy window displays, gardens, street fairs and fountains. After taking a "kur" at 17:00, dine at 20:00 and finish the evening bestowing upon yourself a royal title and promenading down the famous Lichtentaler Alley. (This is lit at night. During the day consider taking the city bus to Kloisterplatz and walking its entire length back into town).

Tomorrow morning, even if you don't gamble, tour the casino. It's open for gambling from 14:00-6:00 (5 DM entry, 10 DM minimum bet, tie and coat required) but gives dicey tours of its Versailles-rivalling interior every morning from 9:30 to 12:00 (2 DM and no ties!)

The Germans who come to Baden-Baden generally stay put for two weeks and the T.I. has enough recommended walks and organized excursions to keep even the most energetic vacationers happy.

▲▲▲ **The Roman-Irish Bath**—The highlight of most Baden-Baden visits is a sober two-hour ritual called the Roman-Irish Bath. Friedrichsbad, on Romerplatz 1, pampered the rich and famous in its elegant surroundings when it opened 150 years ago. Today this steamy world of marble, brass columns, tropical tiles, herons, lily pads, and graceful nudity welcomes gawky tourists as well as locals.

For 25 DM you get the works. The routine is explained in the English brochure and on the walls, following the red arrows: shower to clean—5 minutes; warm air bath, 54 degrees Celsius for 15 minutes; hot air bath, 68 degrees for five minutes; shower; soap brush massage—rough, slippery and finished with a spank; 8 minute shower; thermal steam bath #1, 45 degrees for 10 minutes; thermal steam bath #2, 48 degrees for 5 minutes; thermal bath #3, 36 degrees for 10 minutes; thermal jet spray bath, 34 degrees for 15 minutes; thermal exercise bath, 28 degrees for 5 minutes; shower; cold plunge for 10 seconds; dry in warmed towels for 4 minutes; wrapped like a cocoon on a lounge chair in the silent rest room—30 minutes. Actually, you'll probably get lost about halfway through but don't worry. Linger in the various thermal baths and saunas until you're melted. Don't miss the cold plunge, and steep clean and almost new-born in the silence room. You'll get a key, locker, and towels. The attendants are used to clumsy tourists and speak enough English. Youth hostelers can pick up a 5 DM discount coupon at the hostel. Open Mon 8:00-22:00, Tues 8:00-16:00, Wed 8:00-16:00 and 16:00-22:00 mixed, Sat 8:00-12:00, and 12:00-22:00 mixed, Sun closed. The nearby more modern Caracalla baths are open Sundays. The dress code is always nude. "Mixed" means men and women together. Being a prude, I'm not used to nude. But naked, bewildered and surrounded by beautiful people with no tan lines is a feeling Woody Allen could write a movie about. And it's a great equalizer. I didn't even recognize a striking Parisian woman with diamond studded hair and dressed to kill who had dazzled me earlier out on the streets.

Afterwards, browse through the special exhibits and Roman artifacts in the gallery, sip just a little terrible but "magic" water from the elegant fountain, and stroll down the broad royal stairway feeling, as they say, "five years younger," — or at least no older.

Lodging
Except for its hostel, rooms in Baden-Baden are fairly expensive. But the T.I. can always find you a room if you arrive by 17:00. Private zimmers require longer stays. Take advantage of Baden-Baden's great new **Werner Dietz Youth Hostel** at Hardbergstrasse 34, bus 1 or 3 to Grosse Dollenstrasse, tel 07221/52223, open 8:00-23:30, always saves 30 beds to be doled out to "travelers" at 17:00, 16 DM including sheets, extra in a double room, overflow hall when all beds are taken, 5 DM discount coupons for bath, good meals.

DAY 19

BADEN-BADEN TO THE MOSEL VALLEY

After touring one of the world's most lavish casinos, we'll leave
Baden-Baden for a look at Germany's oldest town, Roman Trier,
and an afternoon meandering through the village vineyards
and soothing views of the Mosel River Valley.

Suggested Schedule

9:30	Tour Baden-Baden casino.
11:00	Drive to Trier with possible stop in Heidelberg or Trier.
15:00	Mosey up the Mosel Valley.
17:00	Find zimmer in Zell.
Sleep	Zell am Mosel

Transportation
From Baden-Baden there's no direct road to Trier. Your fastest
and easiest bet is to remember that in Germany the shortest
distance between any two points is the autobahn, and hook
around past Karlsruhe, Ludwigshafen and Kaiserslautern. From
Trier follow the signs to the Mosel Valley letting the scenic riverside route 53 wind you north past Bernkastel-Kues to Zell am
Mosel.

Eurailers should rearrange things a bit, expressing to Koblenz
(Baden-Baden to Koblenz, changing in Mannheim, two per
hour, two-hour ride) and training down the Mosel to Trier
(hourly, 75-minute rides) or skipping Trier and setting up in
Cochem (on the Trier line).

Sightseeing Highlights
Heidelberg—This famous old university town attracts hordes
of Americans and any former charm is stained almost beyond
recognition by commercialism. If you must see it don't let
yourself—you've seen much better on this trip.
Speyer—You'll be going right by it—and if you'd like to see
Germany's most impressive Romanesque cathedral, drop in.
▲▲ Trier—Germany's oldest city lies at the head of the scenic
Mosel Valley, near the border of Luxembourg. Founded by
Augustus in 15 BC, it was 80,000 strong when Constantine's
father used the town as the capital of the fading Western Roman
Empire. A short stop here offers you a look at Germany's oldest
Christian church and its oldest Gothic church (Dom and Lieb-
frau churches, open 6:00-12:00 and 14:00-17:30). Also, you'll

find Karl Marx's house (fascinating to Marx fans, 15 minute film at :20 past each hour, Tues-Sun 10:00-18:00, Mon 13:00-18:00).

Trier has a lovely park featuring the remains of a Roman bath and the striking 4th century relics of the Roman Emperor's summer residence now built into a palace and church. The famous and huge Porta Nigra (best Roman fortifications in Germany, climb to the top) is noteworthy, but skip the city museum in the adjacent courtyard. The Hauptmarkt square is a pleasant swirl of fruit stands, flowers, painted facades and fountains — with a handy public w.c. Trier's tourist office next to the Porta Nigra is open Mon-Sat 9:00-18:00, Sun 9:00-13:00, tel 0651/75440, when closed a coin-op machine dispenses maps and room lists.

▲▲▲ **Mosel Valley**—The Mosel is what many visitors hoped the Rhine would be—peaceful, sleepy, romantic, with fine wine, plenty of castles and hospitable little towns with lots of zimmers. Boat, train and car traffic here is a trickle compared to the roaring Rhine. While the Mosel flows from France to Koblenz where it dumps into the Rhine, the most scenic piece of the valley lies between the towns of Bernkastel-Kues and Cochem. I'd savor only this section.

Bernkastel, while pretty, is overrated and overcrowded, but the vine-draped castle-studded hills and the meandering Mosel north of there are lovely. The town of Zell am Mosel is best for an overnight stop—peaceful, with a fine riverside promenade, a pedestrian bridge over the river and plenty of zimmers, colorful shops, restaurants, and winestubes.

Further downstream, Beilstein is the quaintest of all Mosel towns. Check out its narrow lanes, ancient wine cellar and ruined castle.

Cochem, with its majestic castle and picturesque Medieval streets, is the touristic hub of this part of the river. Even with its tourist crowds, it's worth a stop. The Cochem castle is spectacular—even if it's the work of over-imaginative 19th century restorers (March 15-Nov 15 9:00-17:00, tours on the hour 3 DM). Consider a boat ride from Cochem to Beilstein (1 hour) or to Zell (3 hours).

Berg Eltz is my favorite castle—possibly in all of Europe. Set in a mysterious forest, left intact for 700 years, furnished throughout as it was 500 years ago, it's a must (April-Oct, Mon-Sat 9:00-17:30, Sun 10:00-17:30, 4.50 DM, by train walk from Moselkern station, midway between Cochem and Koblenz).

Eurailers have some interesting transportation options along the river. While the train can take you along much of the river, consider riding the KD line (Koln-Dusseldorf) which sails from Trier to Bernkastle-Kues and from Cochem to Koblenz (free with Eurail). You can also rent bikes at some stations leaving

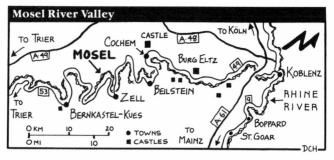

them at others or rent a bike from Zenz at Enderstrasse 3 in
Cochem. If you find yourself stranded in some town, hitching
isn't bad.

Throughout the region on summer weekends, you'll find
wine festivals with oom-pah bands, dancing, colorful costumes
and lots of good food and wine. Any local T.I. can give you a
schedule.

Lodging

Zell is my choice for the evening. The tourist office (next to the
Rathaus) posts room vacancies even after it closes. During my
August visit, 80% of the town's zimmers had beds available. Try
the home of Fritz Mesenich—quiet, friendly, clean, central,
across from a good winestube, 25 DM singles, 40 DM doubles
with breakfast (as usual), Oberstrasse 3, 5583 Zell/Mosel, tel
06542/4753.

For a cozier town farther north, sleep in one of Beilstein's
many zimmers. The T.I. (02673/1417, or 7912 in the winter) is
open daily from 7:00-19:00 in the Cafe Klapperburg.

If you yearn for the closest thing around to a big city, sleep in
Cochem. It has plenty of zimmers on Oberbachstrasse and
Endertstrasse and a youth hostel over the bridge and left half a
mile down Bergstrasse (02671/8633, 9 DM). The Cochem T.I.
(tel 02671/3971, open Mon-Thurs 8:00-17:30, Fri 8:00-19:00,
Sat and Sun 10:00-13:00, 14:00-17:00) books rooms, too.

DAY 20

MOSEL VALLEY TO BONN

After touring the town of Cochem and the great Eltz Castle, we'll travel up to the Rhine and over to the home of West Germany's government and Beethoven—Bonn.

Suggested Schedule	
9:00	Cochem, skip castle, buy picnic.
10:30	Berg Eltz, picnic after tour.
13:30	Drive rest of Mosel, autobahn from Koblenz to Bonn.
16:00	Park near station, visit T.I., get set up. Evening free.
Sleep	Bonn

Transportation
You can't get lost if you stick to the river. For Berg Eltz drive to the car park at the end of the road above Moselkern, or if you'd like to skip the enchanting but long 30-minute walk to the castle, drive around through Lasserg and Wierscheim. The quickest way to Bonn is to enter the autobahn where it crosses the Mosel (Koblenz-Dieblich) and head north following the signs to Koln and Bonn. For a look at Koblenz, Remagen and the capital buildings in Bonn-Bad Godesberg, follow the Mosel into Koblenz, work your way to the Deutsches-Ecke where the rivers touch, then leave town on highway 9 along the Rhine through Mulheim, Andernach, and Remagen.

In Bonn, take the "Bonn-Endenich" exit and follow signs to "zentrum," "stadt-mitte," "bahnhof" and T.I. Park near the bahnhof, there's a big lot just north on Thomastrasse.

By train simply change in Koblenz, catching one of many expresses to Bonn and Koln. (Don't get off in Bonn-Bad Godesberg).

Sightseeing Highlights
Koblenz—Not a nice city, but its historic Deutsches Eck (German corner), the tip of land where the Mosel joins the Rhine, has a certain magnetism. (Koblenz means "confluence" in Latin, the town has Roman origins). Walk through the park, notice the blackened base of what was once a huge memorial to the Kaiser. Across the river, the yellow fortress is now a youth hostel with all the comfort of a WWI trench.

Remagen—Just to the north are the remains of the "Bridge at Remagen" of World War II fame. Not much remains but the memorial and the bridge stubs are enough to stir the emotions of Americans who remember when it was the only remaining bridge that allowed the Allies to cross the Rhine and race to Berlin in 1945. Never closed. Just follow the signs, it's a small town.

Bonn-Bad Godesberg—This suburb of Bonn is the home of West Germany's government. Very little is open to the public, but as you're driving into Bonn on highway 9, you'll go right by the parks, monuments, embassies, and important buildings that make up a national capital.

▲▲ Bonn—Bonn was chosen as West Germany's temporary capital after WWII when German unity was still in the cards. Its sleepy, peaceful nature seemed like a good place to plant Germany's first post-Hitler government. Today it is sleek, modern, and by big city standards, remarkably pleasant and easy going. We're stopping here not to see Beethoven's house or the parliament buildings (neither are very interesting) but to come up for a breath of the real world before finishing off this tour on the misty romantic Rhine.

The T.I., directly in front of the station, is excellent (8:00-21:00, Sun 9:30-12:30, tel 0228/773466, free room finding service). Stop here for info, to confirm tomorrow's plans, and to get advice on overnight parking.

The market square and Munsterplatz are a joy as is the local shopping and people-watching.

Lodging
Hotels are expensive in Bonn but the T.I. is very helpful, and—unlike just about anywhere else we've been—July and August are the least crowded months, since the government takes a summer break.

A great value is the **Hotel Eschweiler**, perfectly located just off the market square on a pedestrian street next to Beethoven's place (ten-minute walk from the station—don't drive). The family that owns and runs the place charges 60 DM for a double (70 DM with a shower), speaks English, and keeps a parakeet in the breakfast room. Bonngasse 7, 5300 Bonn 1, tel 0228-635385.

DAY 21

BONN, KOLN AND THE RHINELAND

Today we get a good dose of no-nonsense urban German muscle, visit its greatest Gothic cathedral along with one of her finest art museums and drive back into the fairytale world of Rhine legends and castles.

Suggested Schedule	
9:00	Catch boat to Koln, see cathedral, museums, train back to Bonn.
13:00	Lunch, afternoon free in Bonn.
16:00	Drive south to Bacharach.
Sleep	Bacharach

Transportation
Big city driving is something most normal people try to minimize. Today we can avoid it entirely by riding the boat up to Koln and returning by train (or vice versa, train ride—7 DM, 4 per hour, 20-minute ride. Ask at the T.I. for boat schedules. All the important sights in each town are within comfortable walking distance between the train and boat stations. Plan this upon arrival in Bonn at the T.I.). If you decide to drive to Koln, park in the pay lot under the cathedral.

From Bonn catch the autobahn south (direction Frankfurt), getting off in downtown Koblenz and following the highway 9 signs in the direction of Mainz. ("Umleitung" is a common road sign around here, it means "detour.") Highway 9 will put you right on the Rhine's west bank. Now the castle fun begins.

Eurailers should train from Bonn through Koblenz to Boppard, a good place to catch one of the KD boats. If you're rushed, stay on the train to whatever Rhine village you choose to call home. Express trains don't stop in small towns so you'll probably be changing trains in Koblenz. The walk from the Koblenz bahnhof to the boat dock is much longer than in the smaller towns further south.

Sightseeing Highlights
▲▲ **Koln (Cologne)**—This big no-nonsense city—Germany's fourth largest—has a tight and fascinating center. Since the Rhine was the northern boundary of the Roman Empire, Koln, like most of these towns, goes back 2,000 years. It was an important cultural and religious center throughout the Middle Ages. Even after WWII bombs destroyed 95% of the city, it re-

mains, after a remarkable recovery, a cultural and commercial center as well as a fun and colorful city.

Its Dom, or cathedral, is far and away Germany's most exciting Gothic church. 50 yards from the station, tours Mon—Fri at 10:00, 11:00, 13:30, 15:30, and 14:30, Sat at 10:00 and 11:00. Next to the Dom is the outstanding Romisch-Germanisches Museum, this tour's best Roman museum (Tues-Sun 10:00-17:00, Wed and Thurs till 20:00, you can view its prize piece, a fine mosaic floor, free, from the front window). Sadly, the displays are in German only. The Wallrof-Richartz Museum has a fine new home between the Roman museum and the river. If you like modern and pop art, don't miss it. (Tues-Sun 10:00-17:00, Tues and Thurs 10:00-20:00, tel 0221/2212379). The T.I. near the station, opposite the Dom's main entry, is very helpful—tel 0221/2213345, daily 8:00—22:30.

Charlemagne's Capital, **Open Air Folk Life**, and **Phantasialand**—If you have an extra day, a number of interesting sights are within easy striking distance of Bonn and Koln. Aachen is a very historic town—the capital of Europe in 800 AD, when Charles the Great called it Aix-le-Chapelle. The remains of his rule are there including a very impressive Byzantine/Ravenna-inspired church with his sarcophagus and throne. The city also has a headliner newspaper museum and great fountains including a clever arrange-'em-yourself version.

If you'd like to learn more about regional folklife, visit the Rheinisches Freilichtmuseum (open air museum) in a lovely natural setting near Kommern (take the Euskirchen—Wisskirchen autobahn exit southwest of Bonn).

And if you'd like to fight the lowbrow local crowds at a tacky second-rate local Disneyland, visit Phantasialand. It's popular enough to have its very own autobahn exit south of Bruhl between Bonn and Koln.

Food and Lodging
Where to stay on the Rhine is a wonderful problem. There are so many fine choices. Every town has plenty of zimmers and gasthauses offering beds for 20 to 25 DM per person. For cheaper beds there are several special youth hostels. And each town has a helpful T.I. eager to set you up. Finding a room should be easy any time of year. St Goar, Bacharach and Oberwesel are the best towns for an overnight stop.

In St Goar I stay one mile north of town in the friendly riverside **Hotel Landsknecht** (tel 06741/1693). Klaus Nickenig and family offer doubles for 75 DM and a classy Rhine terrace. In town, and easier for those without wheels, is **Hotel Montag** (Heerstrasse 128, just across the street from the world's largest free hanging cuckoo clock, tel 1629, all new rooms, 80 DM doubles). Mannfred Montag and his family speak English and run a good shop (especially for steins) adjacent. The best 25 DM hotel beds in town are at **Gasthofe Stadt St Goar** (Pumpengasse 5, tel 1646, near station) and **Gasthof Weingut Muhlenschenke** (actually a small winery with tasting for 6 DM), your best cozy out-of-town bed (Grundelbach 73, tel 1698, 27 DM per person). St Goar's best **zimmers** are the homes of Frau Wolters (Schlosberg 24, tel 1695, on the road to the castle, great view, cozy, 20 DM), Frau Kurz (Ulmenhlf 11, tel 459, 2 minutes from the station, 24 DM), and Frau Schwarz (Heerstrasse 86, tel 7585, very central, on the river, only one room, call first, very very homey, almost too homey, 20 DM). The St Goar **hostel** is a big white building under the castle, run very Germanly, and is a good value with $5 beds and good $4 dinners, tel 06741/388.

The town of Bacharach, near St Goar, has Germany's best youth hostel—a castle on the hilltop with a royal Rhine view. **Jugendherberg Stahleck**, closed from 9:00-17:00, members of all ages welcome, 12.50 DM per bed, normally places available in July and Aug, tel 06743-1266, ten-minute climb on trail from town church or drive up. These **zimmers** are central, charge about 20 DM and speak some English. The homes of: Gerturd Aman (Oberstrasse 13, tel 1271), Annelie Dettmar (Oberstrasse 18, tel 2979), Kathe Jost (Bluchirstrasse 33, tel 1717), Christel Ketzer (Blucherstrasse 51, tel 1617). My choice for the best combination of comfort, hotel privacy with zimmer warmth, central location and medieval atmosphere, is the friendly **Hotel Kranenturm** run by Kurt and Fatima Engel. This is actually part of the medieval fortification, and former towers are now round rooms. Located near the train tracks (ask Kurt to explain his special windows to you) at Langstrasse 30, tel 06743/1308. Great cooking and a Kranenturn ice cream special that may ruin you. 25 DM/person. For atmospheric dining elsewhere in Bacharach try the **Altes Haus**, the oldest building in town.

Oberwesel, an underrated town with a wine fest the second week of Sept, has a friendly T.I. (tel 06744-8131) and a super modern **Youth Hostel** behind the castle, a 20-minute walk from town (They speak English and will hold rooms, tel 06744/8355, pool, 4, 2 and 1-bed rooms 11 DM—22 DM, good meals). **Hotel Goldener Pfropfenzieher** (Am Plan 1, tel 207) is old, creaky and hotelish with doubles costing 60 DM and up. A good zimmer is the home of **Anni Rheinbay** at Liebrfrauchstrasse 42, friendly, central, great value at 20 DM/person.

DAY 22

THE RHINE AND ITS CASTLES
FLY HOME FROM FRANKFURT

A fitting finale for this tour is a day on the Romantic Rhine. We'll
cruise the most exciting stretch and climb through the Rhine-
land's greatest castle before returning, if necessary, to the Frankfurt airport to catch our flight home.

Suggested Schedule	
9:00	Boat to St. Goar, explore Reinfels Castle, buy picnic.
12:00	Boat back to Bacharach.
13:00	Picnic in park. Afternoon free.
	Return to Frankfurt, turn in car and fly home.

Transportation
Today's tempo is dictated by your post-tour plans. If your flight
leaves after 15:00 you can easily take the cruise and tour the
castle. If it leaves earlier, do the cruise and castle on Day 21.
And, if you can spend another night here, this can be a leisurely
day. Eurailers will find handy overnight trains leaving Frankfurt
for Berlin, Copenhagen, Paris, or London.
     Rather than bog down on times, I'll just explain general
possibilities. While trains stop about hourly even in the small
towns, zipping travelers north or south, the most enjoyable way
to experience the valley is on a KD steamer. These run in both
directions several times a day stopping at nearly every village.
Here is a partial KD schedule for boats running daily from June
16 to Sept 15. A complete, and more complicated, schedule is
in the back of this book.

Koblenz to Bingen:

Koblenz		9:00	11:30
Boppard	9:00	10:40	13:15
St Goar	10:15	11:55	14:40
Bacharach	11:20	12:55	15:45
Bingen	12:55	14:20	17:10

Bingen to Koblenz:

Bingen	10:10	10:45	12:35	14:15	16:35
Bacharach	10:55	11:30	13:25	15:05	17:20
St Goar	11:35	12:00	14:10	15:50	18:00
Boppard	12:35	12:50	15:10	16:45	18:50
Koblenz	13:50	14:05	16:25	18:00	20:00

Koblenz to Bingen costs 41 DM. Boppard to Bacharach is 20 DM. Eurailers travel free. Groups of 15 get a 20% discount. Reservations are never necessary but always call or ask locally to confirm your plans.

Taking the boat one way and returning by train is logical. Trains leave major towns almost hourly, and rides are very quick (St Goar—Bacharach 12 min., Bacharach—Mainz 30 min., Mainz—Frankfurt 30 min.)

There's a lovely bike path down the river, but contrary to some sources, you can't rent bikes at stations. While there are no bridges between Koblenz and Mainz, several small ferries do the job nicely.

If you are rushed, the speediest schedule is: tour Rheinfels castle from 9:00 to 10:00, cruise from St Goar to Bacharach from 10:15 to 11:20, picnic in Bacharach and catch the 12:42 train to Frankfurt arriving at 14:05.

Sightseeing Highlights along the Rhine (working south from Koblenz)

Stoltzenfelds Castle—Just south of Koblenz past the huge brewery you'll see this yellow castle. It's a steep 10-minute climb from the mini car park directly below, for a great castle interior. Open 9:00-13:00, 14:00-18:00, closed Mondays.

Marksburg—Across the river from the village of Spey, you'll see the best preserved castle on the Rhine, Marksburg. It has a mandatory tour in German only and they put the castle on the wrong side of the river. It makes a exciting photograph, though.

▲ **Boppard**—Worth a stop. Park near the center (or at the DB train station and walk). Just above the market square are the remains of a Roman wall (we've seen better). On the square, buy the little Mainz-Koblenz guidebook (4.50 DM) with a map. This describes every castle and town we'll see. Below the square is a fascinating church. Notice the carved Romanesque crazies at the doorway. Inside, to the right of the entrance, you'll see Christian symbols from Roman times. Also notice the painted arches and vaults—originally most Romanesque churches were painted this way. On the arches near the river note the high water ("hoch wasser") marks from various flood years.

▲▲ **Rheinfels Castle**—This mightiest of Rhine castles is an intriguing ruin today. Follow the castle map with English instructions (50 pf at the ticket window) through the castle. If you follow the castle's perimeter, circling behind, you'll find a few of the several miles of spooky tunnels—explore. (A flashlight would be handy). Be sure to see the reconstruction of the castle in the museum to see how much bigger it was before Louis XIV destroyed it. The castle shop sells an excellent children's book called "Father Rhine Tells His Sagas"—the big edition, 10 DM,

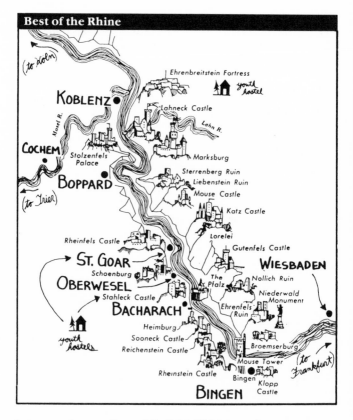

Best of the Rhine

(to Köln) · KOBLENZ · Mosel R. · Ehrenbreitstein Fortress · youth hostel · Lahneck Castle · Lahn R. · COCHEM · Stolzenfels Palace · Marksburg · (to Trier) · BOPPARD · Sterrenberg Ruin · Liebenstein Ruin · Mouse Castle · Katz Castle · Lorelei · Rheinfels Castle · ST. GOAR · Gutenfels Castle · WIESBADEN · Schoenburg · OBERWESEL · The Pfalz · Nollich Ruin · Stahleck Castle · BACHARACH · Niederwald Monument · Ehrenfels Ruin · Heimburg · Sooneck Castle · Reichenstein Castle · Broemserburg · youth hostels · Mouse Tower · (to Frankfurt) · Rheinstein Castle · Bingen · Klopp Castle · BINGEN

has great pictures. Open daily 9:00-18:00, ten minutes steep hike up from St Goar.

St Goar—A pleasant town with good shops (steins and cuckoo clocks, of course), waterfront park and a helpful T.I.

Loreley—This big rock—the ultimate Rhine-stone—is famous for its legendary nymph who used to distract sailors causing them to run aground. (Occasionally, if you listen very carefully, you can still hear her). Any postcard rack will tell you the complete story. This is actually the narrowest part of the Rhine, and a nearby reef makes things even more exciting. There's nothing on the rock except a German flag.

▲ **Bacharach**—Just a very pleasant old town that misses most of the tourist glitz. Next to the KD dock is a great park for a picnic. Herr Kruger in the T.I. is insistently helpful (open Mon-Fri 8:00-12:30, 13:30-17:00, tel 06743/1297, follow signs through a courtyard and up stairs). Some of the Rhine's best wine is from this town.

Mainz, **Wiesbaden**, and **Rudesheim**—Are all too big, too famous, and not worth your time. Mainz's Gutenburg Museum is also a big disappointment. For a note on Frankfurt, look back under Day 1.

Departure Procedure
If you're flying home from Frankfurt be sure to telephone your airline three days in advance to confirm your seat. Also, call the morning of your departure to check the departure time.

To get to the airport by autobahn, head toward Frankfurt. After you cross the Rhine, follow signs to "Flughafen." The airport ("Flughafen") is right on the autobahn and there are plenty of signs to direct you.

By train it's even easier. Train to the Frankfurt central station and follow the signs again to "Flughafen." There's an airport shuttle train every ten minutes and you'll be there in twelve.

As you charge down the runway, with your seatbelt fastened and your dreams in their upright and locked position, I hope you'll enjoy thinking back over a smooth and exciting 22 days in Germany, Switzerland and Austria.

POST-TOUR OPTION

BERLIN

No tour of Germany is complete without a look at its historic capital—Berlin. And it's not included! My greatest frustration in putting this 22 day plan together was my inability to work Berlin in. If you have a couple of extra days, take the easy overnight train ride from Frankfurt and experience the soul of old Germany and the pain of modern Germany.

Suggested Schedule—Berlin in 2 Days

Day 1

7:00	Arrive (overnight trains arrive early), at Berlin's Zoo Bahnhof station.
8:00	Get set up—stop by T.I., get room, move in.
9:00	K'dam—visit Memorial church, tour Ka-De-We Department store, buy picnic.
11:30	Picnic on grounds of Charlottenburg Schloss.
12:00	Tour Palace, cross the street for museum, see Nefertiti.
15:00	Dahlem Museum complex, tour picture gallery.
17:00	Back to hotel to rest, or relax at Wannsee, take a cruise?
19:00	Dinner (Turkish?) near Savignyplatz or on K'dam.
21:00	Sample Berlin nightlife (or watch it) on K'dam.

Day 2

8:00	Breakfast, consider checking out of hotel, store bag at station.
9:00	Stroll through Tiergarten, climb Siegessaule for good E & W view, visit Reichstag History Museum. (Consider hour walk along from Brandenburg to Charlie via Potsdamerplatz).
11:00	Haus am Checkpoint Charlie Museum.
12:30	Walk over wall, Checkpoint Charlie, standup lunch near Unter den Linden.
14:00	Museuminsel—Pergamon Museum.
16:00	Explore people's center—Palast der Republic.
17:00	Changing of guard at Monument to Victims, eternal flame (unless Wed., 14:30).
17:30	Museum of German History.
19:00	Stroll Unter den Linden to Brandenburg Gate.
20:00	Dinner at fast food stand near Fernsehturm.
21:00	Cross back to west, subway to Bahnhof to catch west-bound train.

Getting There

The government subsidizes flights into Berlin (PanAm, British Air and Air France charge as little as $50 from several German cities) and driving in is a simple matter of buying a 6 DM transit visa at the border and autobahning straight through East Germany, but I'd recommend the overnight train in and out from and to Frankfurt at the end of your trip after turning in your rental car.

The night train from Frankfurt (22:35 to 6:13) costs 157 DM round trip second class plus 23 DM for the sleeper (couchette). Buy it round trip with reservations as soon as you are sure of the dates (i.e., in Munich). With a Eurailpass, buy only the East German segment (126 DM, or $63 US round trip) and the couchette reservation if you like. Your East German transit visa is issued free on the train.

Berlin Sightseeing

Kurfurstendamm—The glitter of the crazy 20s echoes here, pampered by economic subsidies from the west, this thriving Champs-Elysees of Germany is a great place to feel the pulse of Berlin—capitalist and determined to be western, K'dam is the heart of the new West Berlin. At the head of K'dam is the main station, Europa Center, Kaiser Wilhelm memorial church and Savignyplatz.

Kaiser-Wilhelm Gedachtiskirche (memorial church)— This most important WWII memorial, with charred and gutted ruins of the old bombed out church, has great ceiling mosaics. Next to it is the very impressive new church. Go inside for a world of blue glass. You'll see why they call this complex the broken tooth, lipstick and the powder compact.

Schloss Charlottenburg—This is the only surviving Hohenzollern Palace and Berlin's top baroque palace. Open Tues-Sun, 9:00-16:00, (bus 54 from Zoo, mandatory tours, in German only) in a pleasant royal garden. Across the street is the Egyptian Museum worth a wander if only to look into the eyes of the elegant 3,000-year-old bust of Queen Nefertiti, from the days of King Tut.

Dahlem Museum—Actually a cluster of important museums that those with an unending appetite for art and culture could spend an entire trip in. Seven museums, all free and open Tues-Sun, 9:00-17:00, bus 1, 10, or 68 or U-Bahn to Dahlem-Dorf. Most important is the Gemaldegalerie (Picture Gallery) with over 600 canvases by Durer, Titian, Botticelli, Rubens, Vermeer, Bruegel, and the world's greatest collection of Rembrandts including the "fake" but lovely "Man with the Golden Helmet."

The Reichstag—The old parliament building, burned by Hitler to frame the communists, now houses a fine modern

Germany history exhibit. History buffs will enjoy comparing
this with the perspective from the left shown in East Berlin's
counterpart. Nearby is the historic Brandenburg Gate and
a good view of the wall. Open 10:00—17:00, Tues—Sun, free.
Take bus 69 from Zoo, the only English film is at 14:00 daily.
The Wall—This 100 mile border erected almost overnight by
East Germany (and friends) in 1961 is thirteen feet high with
a sixteen foot tank ditch and one hundred sixty feet of no man's
land. The opposite of a medieval rampart, this keeps people.
Once called the Anti-Fascist Protective Rampart by the East, still
called disgusting by most in the West, this wall defines Berlin
today—and is a fascinating tourist sight. View it from a platform
on the desolate Potsdamer Platz (the former Times Square of
Berlin), mid-way on a grey and eery walk from Brandenburg
Gate to Checkpoint Charlie.

Don't miss the fascinating Haus am Checkpoint Charlie, the
little museum that tells the history of the wall, imaginative
escape attempts and all. (U-Bahn to Kochstrasse, just before
you cross at Checkpoint Charlie, open daily 9:00-22:00).
Honorable Mention Sights:

Zoo—The world's largest (and possibly the best) zoo stretch-
es out from Berlin's central station. (9:00-17:00, entrance fee,
feeding times posted at entry, morning is the best visiting time).
Next to the zoo is Berlin's biggest and most pleasant city park,
the "Tiergarten."

Gedenksstatte Plotzensee Memorial—Powerful memorial
to Nazi victims in Hitler's former execution chambers.

Bauhaus Archiv-Museum—Popular with architects and
fans of modern design.

Siegessaule—Memorial tower, climb it 285 steps for a good
view of East and West.

EATING

The local cusine is heavy and hearty. While it's tasty, it can get monotonous if you fall into the schnitzel or wurst and potatoes rut. To eat well, use a phrase book or menu translator and be adventurous. Each region has its local specialities which, while not the cheapest, are often the best values on the menu.

There are many kinds of restaurants. Hotels often serve fine food. a "Gaststatte" is a simple less expensive restaurant. The various regions' many ethnic restaurants provide a welcome break from the basic Germanic fare. Foreign food is either from the remnants of a crumbled empire (Hungarian and Bohemian— where Austria gets its goulash and dumplings) or a new arrival to serve the many hungry but poor guest workers. Italian, Turkish, Greek and Yugoslavian food in Germany and Switzerland is commonplace and a good value. Chinese food and "new cuisine" from France and Italy are more and more popular. The cheapest meals are found in department store cafeterias, "Schnell-Imbiss" (fast food) standup joints, university cafeterias (called "mensas,"-tourists welcome) and at youth hostels.

Most restaurants tack a menu onto their door for browsers— and will have either an English menu or someone who can translate for you. Even so, sooner or later you'll be rudely surprised as I was when my "pepperoni" pizza arrived covered with green peppers. Service is normally included although it's customary to round the bill up after a good meal.

For most visitors the rich pastries, the wine and the beer provide the fondest memories of Germany's cuisine. The wine, mostly white, is particularly good from the Mosel, Rhine, Danube, east Austria, and southwest Switzerland areas. Order wine by the "viertel" or quarter liter. You can say "Ein viertel suss" (sweet), "halbe trochen" (medium) or "trochen" (dry) "weiss" (white) or "rot" (red) "wein" (wine) "bitte" (please).

The Germans enjoy a tremendous variety of great beer. The average German, who drinks forty gallons of beer a year, knows that "dunkel" is dark, "hell" is light, "flaschenbier" is bottled and "vom fass" is on tap. "Pils normales" is barley-based, "weize" is wheat based and "malzbier" is the malt beer that children learn on. When you order beer, ask for "ein halb" for a half liter or "ein mass" for a whole liter. Some beerhalls only serve it by the liter.

ACCOMMODATIONS

While accommodations in Germany, Switzerland, and Austria are fairly expensive they are normally very comfortable and a good value. Plan on spending $35 per double in big cities, $20 in towns.

I have assumed you'll be needing doubles and the prices listed are for doubles (including breakfast). The more people you put in a hotel room, the cheaper it gets. While hotel singles are most expensive, private accommodations (zimmers) have a flat per person rate. Hostels and dorms always charge per person. People staying several nights are most desirable. One night stays are sometimes given an extra charge.

The listings in this book are places that I have slept in or reviewed in 1986. In recommending a hotel I like places that are in a convenient, central, quiet and safe location, small, family-run with local character, simple facilities not catering to American "needs," inexpensive, friendly, English-speaking, and clean. Obviously a friendly, clean, quiet, central, cheap room is virtually impossible to find and all of my recommendations fall sort of perfection—sometimes miserably. But I've listed the best values for each price category that I could find, given the above criteria.

While you'll see lots of "no vacancy" signs in July, August, and during a few scattered holiday periods, reservations are not normally necessary. During peak times, or if you have a particular place you want, call ahead or try to arrive early. I've taken great pains to list telephone numbers with long distance instructions. Use the telephone. A hotel receptionist will trust you, holding a room until 5pm. Please don't let these people down. If you say you'll come, come. Or call and cancel.

Accommodations categories in descending order of price are: Hotel, Hotel Garni (room and breakfast only, no other meals), Pension, Gasthof, Fremdenzimmer, Zimmer frei (private home), Youth hostel, camping, and park bench. Room lists are always available at local tourist offices and remaining vacancies are often posted there after hours. Normally the cost of a room includes a continental breakfast, taxes, service, and showers either in the room or down the hall. This price is usually posted in the room. Before accepting confirm that breakfast is included. The only tip the hotels I've listed would like is a friendly, easy-going guest.

Those camping should get a camping guide for the area. You'll find campgrounds just about wherever you need them. Look for "campingplatz" signs. Camping is a popular middle-class family way to go among Germans. You'll find that campgrounds are cheap, friendly, safe, and very rarely full.

Youth hostelers can take advantage of the wonderful network of hostels (see listing later). Follow the signs marked "Jugend-herberge." Triangles and the "tree next to a house" are also youth hostel symbols. Generally you must have your member-ship card ($20 per year, sold in most U.S. cities), though sometimes non-members are admitted for an extra charge.

Hostels are open to members of all ages (except in Bavaria where a 26 year maximum age is strictly enforced). They usually cost $4 to $8 per night (plus sheet rental if you don't have your own), and serve good cheap meals or provide kitchen facili-ties. While many have couple or family rooms, plan on beds in segregated dorms—five to twenty per room. Hostels can be idyllic and peaceful, or school groups can raise the rafters. I like small hostels best.

YOUTH HOSTELS—JUDENDHERBERGE

Listed below are the youth hostels that fall within easy striking distance of our 22 day tour. They are grouped in regions with each hostel's address, phone number, and number of beds listed. For a complete listing of Europe's 2,000 hostels pick up an international directory at any hostel.

ROMANTIC ROAD REGION
Frankfurt—Haus der Jugend, Deutschherrunfer 12, 6000 Frankfurt/Main 70, tel 0611/619058, 500 beds.
Wurzburg—Burkarderstr. 44, 8700 Wurzburg, tel 0931/705913, 150 beds.
Igersheim—Erlenbachtalstr. 44, 6991 Igersheim/b. Bad Mergentheim, tel 07931/6373, 150 beds.
Creglingen—Erdbacherstr. 30, 6993 Creglingen, tel 07933/336, 114 beds.
Weikershrim—Haus der Musik, Im heiligen Wohr, 6992 Weikersheim, tel 07934/7025, 110 beds.
Rothenburg—1) Rossmuhle 8803 Rothenburg/Tauber, tel 0986¼ 510, 141 beds.
   2) Spitalhof, Postfach 1206, 8803 Rothenburg/Tauber, tel 09861/4510, 141 beds.
Feuchtwangen—Dr. Guthlein-Weg 1, 8805 Feuchtwangen, tel 09852/842, 152 beds.
Dinkelsbuhl—Koppengasse 10, 8804 Dinkelsbuhl, tel 09851/509, 150 beds.
Rechenberg—Schloss, Zum Schloss 7, 7181 Stimpfach-Rechtenberg, tel 07967/372, 116 beds.

Nordlingen—Kaiserwiese 1, 8860 Nordlingen, tel 09081/
84109, 80 beds.

Donauworth—Goethestr. 10, 8850 Donauworth, tel
0906/5158, 130 beds.

Munich—1) Wendl-Dietrich Str.20, 8000 Munchen 19,
tel 089/1311560, 510 beds.

2) Jugendgastehaus, Miesingstr. 4, 8000 Munchen 70,
tel 089/7236550, 344 beds.

Pullach (near Munich)—Burg Schwaneck, Burgweg 4-6,
8023 Pullach, tel 089/7932381, 130 beds.

BAVARIA—TYROLIA

Reutte—6600 Reutte, Prof Dengel-Strasse 20, Tirol, tel
05672/3039, 28 beds.

Reutte-Hofen—6600 Reutte, Jugengastehaus am Graben,
Postfach 3, Tirol, tel 05672/2644, 860, 38 beds.

Fussen—Mariahilferstr. 5, 8958 Fussen (Allgau), tel 08362/
7754, 150 beds.

Oberammergau—Malensteinweg 10, 8103 Oberammergau,
tel 08822/4114, 130 beds.

Garmisch-Partenkirchen—Jochstr. 10, 8100 Garmisch-
Partenkirchen, tel 0882/2980, 290 beds.

Mittenwald—Buckelwiesen 7, 8102 Mittenwald, tel 08823/
1701, 140 beds.

Innsbruck—1) 6020 Innsbruck, Reichenauerstr. 147, Tirol,
tel 05222/46179, 190 beds.

2) Studentenheim, 6020 Innsbruck, Reichenauerstr. 147,
tel 05222/46179, 112 beds.

3) 6020 Innsbruck, Rennweg 176, Tirol, tel 05222/25814,
100 beds.

4) 6020 Innsbruck, Sillg 8a, Tirol, tel 05222/31311, 100 beds.

5) 6020 Innsbruck, Volkshaus, Radetzkystr. 47, tel 05222/
466684, 52 beds.

Salzburg/Salzkammergut—1) 5026 Sazburg, Aigner Strasse
34, tel 0662/23248, 19 beds.

2) 5020 Salzburg-Nonntal, Josef-Preis Allee 18, tel 0662/
42670, 360 beds.

3) Eduard-Heinrich-Haus, 5020 Salzburg-Josefau, Eduard-
Heinrich-Str. 2, tel 0662/25976, 153 beds.

4) 5020 Salzburg, Glockengasse 8, tel 0662/76241, 152 beds.

5) 5020 Salzburg, Hannspergstrasse 27, tel 0662/75030,
108 beds.

6) 5020 Salzburg, HausderJugend, Franz Hinterholzer Kai 8,
tel X, 70 beds.

St Gilgen—5340 St Gilgen, Haus Schafbergblick, Mond Seerstr.
7-11, Salzburg, 1 tel 06227/365, 70 beds.

Bad Ischl—4820 Bad Ischl, Am Rechensteg 5, Oberosterreich, tel 06132/2577, 140 beds.
Hallstatt-Lahn—4830 Hallstatt-Lahn 50, Oberosterreich, tel 06134/279, 53 beds.
Gosau—4824 Gosau, Dr Eder-Haus, Oberosterreich, tel 06136/352, 68 beds.
Obertraun—4831 Obertraun, Winkl 26, Oberosterreich, tel 06134/360, 160 beds.
Bad Aussee—8990 Bad Aussee, Lerchenreith 148, Steiermark, tel 06152/2238, 156 beds.

VIENNA/DANUBE
Vienna—1) Jugendgastehaus Wein-Brigittenau, 1200 Wien, Friedrich Engelsplatz 24, tel 0222/338294, 258 beds.
2) 1070 Wien, Myrthengasse 7, tel 0222/936316, 123 beds.
3) 1030 Wien III, Lechnerstrasse 12, tel 0222/731494, 52 beds.
4) Ruthensteiner JH, 1150 Wien XV, Robert Hamerlinggase 24, tel. 0222/834693, 77 beds.
5) 1130 Wien XIII, Jugendhergerge der Stadt Wein (Hutteldorf), Schlossberggasse 8, tel 0222/821501, 273 beds.
Melk—3390 Melk an der Donau, Abt-Karl-Strasse 42, Niederosterreich, tel 02752/2681, 66 beds.

APPENZELL
Appenzell—Schwende-Weissbad, 9057 Weissbad, tel 071/881189, 35 beds.
St. Gallen—Juchstrasse 25/Speicherstrasse, 9000 St Gallen, tel 071/243444, 142 beds.
Wildhaus—Unterwasser-Befang, 9658 Wildhaus (St Gallen), tel 074/51270, 75 beds.
Schaan—Vaduz-untere Ruttigasse 6, 9494 Schaan-Vaduz, tel 075/25022, 104 beds.

INTERLAKEN/JUNGFRAU REGION
Interlaken—Bonigen—Aareweg 21, as See, 3806 Bonigen (Bern), tel 036/224353, 200 beds.
Gimmelwald—Beim Rest Schilthorn, 3801 Gimmelwald (Bern), tel 036/551704, 44 beds.
Grindelwald—Terrassenweg, 3818 Grindelwald (Bern), tel 036/531009, 133 beds.
Brienz—Strandweg 10, am See, 3855 Brienz (Bern), tel 036/511152, 100 beds.

SOUTHWEST SWITZERLAND

Zweisimmen—3770 Zweisimmen-Tull (Bern), tel 030/22188, 130 beds.

Saanen—Chalet Rublihorn, 3792 Saanen, tel 030/41343, 40 beds.

Chateau d'Oex—Les Riavx, 1837 Chateau d'Oex (Baud), tel 029/46404, 52 beds.

Montreaux—Haut Lac, Passage de l'auberge 8, 1820 Territet (Vaud), tel 021/634934, 114 beds.

Lausanne—Chemin du Muguet 1, 1007 Lausanne-ouchy (Vaud), tel 021/265782, 180 beds.

WEST SWITZERLAND

Bern—Jugendhaus, Weihergasse 4, 3005 Bern, tel 031/226316, 144 beds.

Avenches—rue du Lavoir 5, 1580 Avenches (Vaud), tel 037/752666, 78 beds.

Biel—Solothurnerstrasse 137, 2504 Biel (Bern), tel 032/412965, 40 beds.

Neuchatel—rue du Suchiez 35, 2006 Neuchatel, tel 038/257940, 66 beds.

BLACK FOREST

Lorrach—Steinenweg 40, 7850 Lorrach, tel 0762¼ 7040, 163 beds.

Kandern-Platzhof—Auf der Scheideck, 7853 Steinen (Schwarzwald), tel 07626/484, 74 beds.

Wieden—JH Belchen, Oberwieden 16, Am Wiedener Eck 7861 Wieden, tel 07673/538, 176 beds.

Todtnauberg—Fleinerhaus, Radscherstr 12, 7868 Todtnau 2, tel 07671/275, 156 beds.

Feldberg—Hebelhof Passhohe 14, 7821 Feldberg (Schwarzwald), tel 07676/221, 260 beds.

Freiburg—Kartauserstr 151, 7800 Freiburg, tel 0761/67656, 375 beds.

Breisach—Munsterbergstr 30-33, 7814 Breisach (Schwarzwald), tel 07667/7665, 88 beds.

Baden-Baden—Hardberstr 34, 7570 Baden-Baden, tel 07221/52223, 144 beds.

MOSEL

Trier—Maarstr 156, 5500 Trier/Mosel, tel 0651/41092, 312 beds.

Bernkastel-Kues—Jugendherbergsstr. 1, 5550 Bernkastel-Kues/Mosel, tel 06531/2395, 140 beds.

Traven-Trarbach—Am Hirtenpfadchen, 5580 Traven-Trarbach, tel 06541/9278, 190 beds.

Cochem—Klottenerstr 9, 5590 Cochem/Mosel, tel 02671/
8633, 177 beds.
Brodenbach—Moorkamp 7, 5401 Brodenbach/Mosel,
tel 02605/3389, 137 beds.

RHINE
Koln—1) Koln-Riehl, Jugendgastehaus, An der Schanze 14
5000 Koln 60, tel 0221/767081, 366 beds.
 2) Koln-Deutz, Siegesstr 5a, 5000 Koln, 21, tel 0221/814/711,
364 beds.
Bonn—Venusberg, Haager Weg 42, 5300 Bonn 1, (Rheinland),
tel 0228/281200, 276 beds.
Bonn-Bad Godesberg—Jugendgastehaus, Horionstr. 60,
5300 Bonn 2, (Rheinland), tel 0228/317516, 90 beds.
St Goar—Bismarckweg 17, 5401 St Goar, tel 06741/388,
160 beds.
Oberwesel—Jugendgastehaus, Auf dem Schonberg, 6532
Oberwesel, tel 06744/8355, 102 beds.
Bacharach—Jugendburg Stahleck, 6533 Bacharach/Rhein,
tel 06743/1266, 207 beds.
Bingen-Bingerbruck—Herter Str 51, 6530 Bingen 1, Binger-
bruck/Rhein, tel 06721/32163, 194 beds.

COMMUNICATING IN GERMAN

All but two days of this tour are in German-speaking areas. While you'll hear lots of English in touristed areas, train stations, hotels, and in the tourist offices, and you can manage this trip fine speaking only English, a little understanding of German will give your trip a real bonus.

I carried a small dictionary in the glove compartment and a Berlitz German Phrase Book with me most of the time. I also enjoyed a routine of learning (and using) five new words a day. Here are a few tips for the lazy linguist and a list of words I found most useful. When you're in a bind remember the Swiss in general and young people everywhere are most likely to understand your English *if* you keep it clean, simple, and pronounce every letter.

The Germans have a couple of twists to their way of writing and pronouncing. "W" is always pronounced like a "V," and "I" usually sounds like a long "E." "J" is like "Y," "CH" like the "CH" in the Scottish "Loch," "R's" are rolled, "Sch" like "Sh," "tsch" like "ch," "tz" and "z" like "ts" in "sits." They have a letter which looks like our cursive capital "B" and is pronounced like a double "S." Two dots over vowels is an umlaut. These have sounds rare in English. To make an umlaut sound you make your lips round to say "o" but try to say "e". (Out of pure laziness, I've left the umlauts out of this book, sorry.)

An understanding of how English (which is a "Germanic" language), German and Latin relate is very helpful. For instance, English words ending in "ic" are usually Latin. To make that word German, replace the "ic" with "ish." (Barbaric—barbarish, fantastic—fantastish, esoteric—esoterish.) Won't it be fun to be able to say "comic" and "idiotic" on your trip? Also, "ize" English words become "izerin" words auf Deutsch (vocalize—vocalizerin, economize—economizerin).

Germany has some fun combination words. Be on the lookout for words like "Fingerhut"—finger house (thimble), "Halbinsel"—half island (peninsula), and "Stinktier"—stinky animal (skunk).

Each country has a distinct dialect which is difficult for us to hear. The Swiss speak Swiss-German but write High-German like the Germans. They'll greet you with a cheery "Greutzi," say goodbye with a "Ciao" (pron. Jo), and use "Merci" for thank you. Austrians speak a lilting dialect close to Bavarian. People in both regions greet each other with "Gruss Gott" (May God greet you).

German Vocabulary for Travelers

Hello   guten tag
How are you?   Wie geht es?
I'm fine, thanks.   Es geht mir gut, dahnke.
Please   bitte
Thank you   danke schon
See you later   bis bald
Goodnight   gute nacht
Goodbye   auf wiedersehn
Yes/no   ja/nein
Good/bad   gut/schlecht
Beautiful/ugly   schon/hasslich
Big/small   gross/klein
Fast/slow   schnell/langsam
Very   sehr
Enough   genug
How much?   Wieviel?
Money   geld
Cheap/expensive   billig/teuer
Complete price (everything included)   alles ist inbegriffen
I don't understand.   Ich verstehe nicht.
What do you call this?   Wie heisst das?
I'm tired.   Ich bin mude.
I   ich
You   du
Love   liebe
Sleep   schlaf
Friend   freund
Castle   schloss
Valley   tal
Train   zug
Station   bahnhoff
Toilet   klo
Tourist Information   verkehrsamt (or) i
Post and telephone office   PTT
What time is it?   Wieviel uhr ist es?
Yesterday   gestern
Today   huete
Tomorrow   morgen
This evening   heutte abend
Morning   morgen
Rest day   ruhetag
Vacation   urlaub
Where is . . . ?   Wo ist . . . ?
To the right   rechts
To the left   links

I'm lost. Ich habe mich verirrt.
Are you rich and single? Sind sie reich und einzel?
I am rich and single. Ich bin reich und einzel.
Room for rent zimmer (or) zimmerfrei (or) fremdenzimmer (or) gastezimmer
Double bed room doppelbett zimmer
Single room einselbett zimmer
Dormitory schlafsaal (or) lager (or) massen lager (or) matratzenlager
 Without shower (with) ohne dusche (mit)
Holiday apartments (long term only, 5 day minimum) ferienwohnung
No vacancy belegt
Adult erwachsen
Gas—regular benzin
Gas—unleaded bleifrei
Gas—super super
Diesel diesel
Self-service ("'sb" at gas stations) selbstbedienung
Guided tour fuhrung

Numbers

Zero null
One eins
Two zwei
Three drei
Four vier
Five funf
Six sechs
Seven sieben
Eight acht
Nine neun
Ten zehn
Eleven elf
Twelve zwolf
Thirteen dreizehn
Fourteen vierzehn
Fifteen funfzehn
Sixteen sechzehn
Seventeen siebzehn
Eighteen achtgzehn
Nineteen neunzehn
Twenty zwanzig
Twenty-one einundzwanz ig
Twenty-two zweiundzwanzig
Twenty-three dreiundzwanzig
Twenty-four vierunzwanzig

Twenty-five funfundzwanzig
Thirty dreissig
Thirty-five funfunddreissig
Thirty-six sechsunddreissig
Thirty-seven siebenunddrei ssig
Thirty-eight achtunddreissig
Thirty-nine neununddreissig
Forty vierzig
Fifty funfzig
Sixty sechzig
Seventy seibzig
Eighty achtzig
Ninety neunzig
One hundred hundert
One hundred twenty-five hundertfunfundzwanzig
One hundred fifty hundertfunfzig
One hundred seventy-five hundertfunfundseibzig
Two hundred zweihundert
Two hundred fifty zweihundertfunfzig
Three hundred dreihundert
Four hundred vierhundert
Five hundred funfhundert
Seven hundred siebenhundert
One thousand tausend
One thousand one hundred tausendeinhundert
Two thousand zweitausend
Five thousand funftausend
Ten thousand zehntausend

Food Vocabulary

Food Speise
Grocery store Supermarkt
Picnic Picknick
Delicious Lecker
Market Markt
Drunk Betrunken
Cheers! Prosit!
I'm hungry. Ich habe hunger.
Water wasser
Coffee kaffee
Tea tee
Milk milch
Beer bier
Wine wein
Cider obstwein
Lemonade zitronensaft

Hors d'oeuvres   vorspeise
Bread   brot
Soup   suppe
Eggs   eier
Fish   fisch
Lobster   hummer
Meat   fleisch
Beef   rindfleisch
Beefsteak   beefsteak
Pork   schweinefleisch
Ham   Schinken
Mutton   hammelfleisch
Venison   wild
Veal   kalbfleisch
Chicken   huhn
Rice   reis
Potatoes   kartoffein
Vegetables   gemuse
Salad   salat
Tomatoes   tomaten
Cabbage   kohl
Green peas   grune erbsen
Beans   bohnen
Mushrooms   champignons
Cheese   kase
Fruit   fruchte
Pastries   feines geback
Ice cream   eis
Cookies   kekse
Orange   orange
Apple   apfel
Banana   banane
Grapes   weintraube
Pear   birne
Cherries   kirschen
Strawberries   erdbeeren
Sugar   zucker
Cream   sahne
Salt   salz
Pepper   pfeffer
Oil   ol
Vinegar   essig
Mustard   senf
Garlic   knoblauch
Butter   butter
Jam   konfiture
Knife   messer

Fork gabel
Spoon loffel
Bottle flasche
Glass glas
Cup tasse
Plate teller
Napkin serviette
Rare blutig
Medium halbengleich
Well done durch
Warm warm
Cold, iced geeist
Show me the menu. Zeigen sie mir das menu.
I would like. . . Ich mochte. . .
How much is the meal? Was kostet die mahlzeit?
Is service included? Ist die bedienung inbegriffen?
The check, please. Die rechnung, bitte.
Breakfast fruhstuck
Lunch mittagessen
Dinner abendessen
To drink trinken
To eat essen

Place Names. Many are confused by German place names that differ from what we call them in English. Learn these:

West Germany Deutschland, or Bundesrepublik Deutschland (BRD)
Romantic Road Romantische Strasse
Munich Munchen
Bavaria Bayern
Bavarian Bayerisch
Black Forest Schwarzwald
Cologne Koln

East Germany Deutsche Demokratische Republic (DDR)

Austria Osterreich
Vienna Wien
Danube Donau

Switzerland Schweiz
Lake Constance Bodensee
Lake Geneva Lac Leman
Lake Lucerne Lac Luzern

TOURIST INFORMATION (T.I.)

Each of these countries has an excellent network of tourist information offices both locally and in the USA. Before your trip, send a letter to each country's National Tourist Office (listed below) telling them of your general plans and asking for info. They'll send you the general packet and if you ask for specifics (calendars of local festivals, good hikes around Fussen, castle hotels along the Rhine, the wines of Austria, etc.) you'll get an impressive amount of help. If you have a specific problem they are a good source of help.

During your trip your first stop in each town should be the tourist office where you'll take your turn at the informational punching bag smiling behind the desk. This person is rushed and tends to be robotic. Prepare. Have a list of questions and a proposed plan to double check with him or her. They have a wealth of material that the average "Duh, do you have a map?" tourist never taps. I have listed phone numbers throughout, and if you'll be arriving late, or want to arrange a room, call ahead.

The great frustration for us English-speakers is touring great sights with a German-only guided tour. It's much more work for a guide to struggle in English and most don't want to. The most famous sights normally have English tours when 20 or so people gather, or they hand out read-along fliers. Be sure to politely but firmly let your guide know that several people here speak only English and are dying to know more about this place. Then stare hungrily at the guide until a little English info sneaks out as the rest of the group enters behind you or leaves the room.

National Tourist Offices in the USA:

German National Tourist Office
747 3rd Ave, NY NY 10017, 212/308-3300
444 S Flower, Los Angeles CA 90010, 213/688-7332

Austrian National Tourist Office
500 5th Ave., Suite 2009, NY NY 10110, 212/944-6880
11601 Wilshire Blvd., Los Angeles CA, 213/477-3332

Swiss National Tourist Office
608 5th Ave, NY NY 10020, 212/757-5944
250 Stockton St, San Francisco CA 94108, 415/362-2260

TELEPHONING

Too many timid tourists never figure out the phones. They work and are essential to smart travel. Call hotels in advance to make a reservation whenever you know when you'll be in town. If there's a language problem, ask someone at your hotel to talk to your next hotel for you.

Public phone booths are much cheaper than using the more convenient hotel phones. The key to dialing direct is understanding area codes. For calls to other European countries, dial the international access code (00 in Germany, 00 in Switzerland, and 050 in Austria) followed by the country code, followed by the area code without its zero, and finally the local number (4 to 7 digits). When dialing long distance within a country start with the area code (including its zero) then the local number.

Telephoning the USA from a pay phone is easy. Gather a pile of large coins ($2 per minute) and find a booth that says international. The best budget approach is to call with a coin and have that person return your call at a specified time at your hotel. From the USA they'd dial 011-country code-area code without zero-local number. Collect, person to person, credit card calls etc. are more expensive and complicated. Calls from midnight to 8:00am are 20% cheaper but Europe to USA calls are twice as expensive as direct calls from the USA.

City	Area Code	Tourist Info
Frankfurt	0611	231055
Rothenburg	09861	2038
Munich	089	239-1259
Reutte	05672	2336
Salzburg	0662	71712
Hallstatt	06134	208
Vienna	0222	431608
Innsbruck	05222	25715
Hall in Tyrol	05223	6269
Appenzell	071	874111
Interlaken	036	222121
Gimmelwald	036	551955
Montreux	021	631212
Murten	037	715112
Bern	031	227676
Staufen	07633	80536
Baden Baden	07221	275200
Bonn	0228	773466
St Goar	06741	383
Bacharach	06743	1266
Berlin	030	262-6031

Country Codes
USA—1
Canada—1
France—33
Belgium—32
West Germany—49
East Germany—37
Italy—39
Netherlands—31
Switzerland—41
Austria—43
Great Britain—44

International Code to Call Out of:
Germany—00
Austria—050
Switzerland—00

U.S. Embassies or Consulates
Vienna—0222/315511
Munich—089/2301
Bern—031/437011

Train Info
Munich—592991
Vienna—7200
Bern—222404
St Goar—424

Directory Assistance
Germany
Info, local—118 or 0118
International assistance—00118

Switzerland
International directory assistance—191
T.I.—120
Weather—162
Local directory assistance—111

Austria—Vienna
Info, local—15

International assistance—08

MONEY

Germany—Deutsch Marks (DM) are divided into 100 pfennig (pf or p). $1 = 2DM. You'll find 5 pf, 10 pf, 50 pf, 1, 2, and 5 DM coins. Bills come in 10, 20, 50, 100 and 500 denominations.

Austria—Austrian Shilling (AS) are divided into 100 groschen. 14 AS = $1. You'll rarely deal with groschen and shillings come in coins of 1, 5, 10, and 20, bills in 20, 50, 100, 500, and 1000 notes.

Switzerland—The Swiss franc (SF) is divided into 100 centimes. It's a strong currency and about 1.6 SF = $1. You'll find 10 and 20 cent coins along with ½, 1, 2, and 5 SF coins, 10, 20, 50, 100, 500 and 1000 SF bills. The ½ franc coin is often confused with the smaller coins. Notice the ½ franc is the one with ridges on its edge.

DRIVING

This route is ideal by car. Every long stretch is autobahn (super freeway) and nearly every scenic backcountry drive is paved and comfortable. Drivers over 21 need only their USA license and the insurance that comes automatically with your rental car. There are no border formalities to worry about.

The local rules of the road are much like ours. Learn the universal road signs (charts explain them in most road atlases and at service stations). Seatbelts are required and two beers under those belts is enough to land you in jail.

Use local maps and study them before each drive. Familiarize yourself with which exits you need to look out for, which major cities you'll travel in the direction of, where the ruined castles lurk, etc. Pick up the "cardboard clock" (available free at gas stations, police stations and Tabak shops) and display your arrival time on the dashboard so parking attendents can see you've been there less than the posted maximum stay (blue lines indicate 90-minute zones on Austrian streets).

To understand the complex but super-efficient autobahn (no speed limit, toll free) pick up the "Autobahn Service" booklet at any autobahn reststop (free, listing all intersection signs, stops, services, etc). Use a good map, study the intersection signs— "dreiecke" means three corners or a "y" in the road, "autobahn-kreuz" is a "cross" or an intersection. Gas stations are spaced about every 30 miles, normally with a restaurant, small shop, and sometimes a tourist info desk. Exits are often 20 miles apart. Know what you're looking for—nord, sud, ost, west, or mittel—miss it and you'll be long gone. When driving slower than 120 mph, stay out of the left hand passing lane. Remember, in Europe, the shortest distance between any two points is the autobahn. Signs directing you to the autobahn are usually green.

Try to rent a car with a trunk so you can leave "deep storage" things safely out of sight. I keep a box in the trunk for things I don't need to cart in and out of hotels. My pantry box sits on the back seat and I equip it for easy and enjoyable, time- and money-saving car picnics (either at the very pleasant autobahn picnic areas or as I drive—if my navigator can play cook). I stock up with plenty of orange juice in liter boxes, paper towels, plastic cups, and so on. Copy the car key as soon as possible for safety and so two people have access to the car.

Germany, Switzerland, and Austria By Train In 22 Days

Day		Overnight In:
1	Arrive Frankfurt, train to Rothenburg	Rothenburg
2	Sightsee Rothenburg, afternoon Romantic Road bus to Munich	Munich
3	All day Munich	Munich
4	All day Munich, side trip to Dachau	Munich
5	Tour highlights of Bavaria, Mad Ludwig's Castle	Reutte
6	Tyrol, Berchtesgaden, Salzburg	Salzburg
7	Salzburg with side trip into Salzkammergut	Salzburg
8	Early train to Melk, tour abbey, cruise Danube	Vienna
9	All day in Vienna	Vienna
10	All day in Vienna	Night Train
11	Tour Luzern, Ballenberg Folk Museum	Near Interlaken
12	Hike Grindelwald-Kl.Scheidegg-Lauterbrunnen	Gimmelwald
13	Free day to relax in Alps	Gimmelwald
14	Travel to Montreux, Chateau Chillon	Montreux
15	Cruise Lake, visit Lausanne, Murten	Murten
16	Sightsee Bern, into Black Forest	Freiburg
17	Freiburg, Black Forest or Baden-Baden	Freiburg or Baden-Baden
18	Express Train to Cochem via Mannheim and Cochem	Koblenz
19	Explore Mosel, Berg Eltz, set up in Bonn	Bonn
20	Bonn, Koln, set up in Rhineland	Bacharach
21	Cruise Rhine, tour Rheinfels castle	Bacharach
22	Fly home from Frankfurt	

While this itinerary is designed for car travel, it can be adapted for train and bus. The trains cover all the cities very well but can be frustrating in several rural sections. This itinerary would make a three-week first class Eurailpass worthwhile—especially for a single traveler. ($350, available from your travel agent or by mail from Europe Through the Back Door—see catalog page).

Eurailers should know what extras are included on their pass—like any German buses marked "bahn" (run by the train company), boats on the Rhine, Mosel and Danube rivers and the Swiss lakes, and the Romantic Road bus tour. While this itinerary justifies a 21 day ($350) train pass, if you decide to buy tickets as you go, look into local specials. Seniors (women over 60, men over 65) and youths (under 26, Transalpino or BIGE tickets) can enjoy substantial discounts.

Each segment of this plan is explained for Eurailers in the main text. For more information take advantage of the very helpful train station information offices. Tell them what you want to do and they'll tell you how to do it by rail or bus.

A train/bus version of this trip requires some tailoring to avoid areas that are difficult without your own wheels and to take advantage of certain bonuses that train travel offers. Trains in this region are punctual and well organized.

Frankfurt to

Amsterdam CS

4 37	11 14	☒ Köln
6 48	12 14	☒ Duisburg
7 26	13 14	
10 48	16 14	IC ☓ ☒ Duisburg
Ⓐ 11 48	17 14	IC ☓ ☒ Duisburg
12 48	18 14	IC ☓ ☒ Duisburg
13 48	19 14	IC ☓ ☒ Duisburg
14 46	19 59	IC ☓ ☒ Duisburg IC ☓
15 46	20 59	IC ☓
Ⓑ 16 48	22 14	IC ☓ ☒ Duisburg
18 48	0 21	IC ☓ ☒ Duisburg

Berlin Zool. Garten

8 54	16 20	☓
9 24	17 09	IC ☓ ☒ Hannover ☓
11 24	18 47	IC ☓ ☒ Hannover ☓
13 24	20 38	IC ☓ ☒ Hannover ☓
15 33	22 43	
22 35	6 13	⌁ ⊸

København

0 06	12 09	⌁ ⊸ ☒ Hamburg
0 30	14 09	⌁ ⊸ ☒ Hamburg
Ⓢ 8 23	19 29	IC ☓ ☒ Hamburg
9 23	19 45	IC ☓ ☒ Hamburg IC ☓
12 23	22 50	IC ☓ ☒ Hamburg
16 31	6 45	⌁ ⊸

München
continued/suite/Fortsetzung

9 21	13 24	IC ☓
Ⓒ 10 21	14 03	IC ☓
10 50	15 10	☓
11 21	15 24	IC ☓
12 21	16 03	IC ☓
13 21	17 03	IC ☓
14 21	18 27	IC ☓
15 21	19 03	IC ☓
16 21	20 24	IC ☓
Ⓑ 17 21	21 05	IC ☓
18 21	22 05	IC ☓
19 21	23 26	IC ☓
Ⓑ 20 21	0 17	IC ☓ ☒ Würzburg

Ⓒ ①–⑥

Innsbruck to

München

4 45	6 57	
7 40	10 03	
9 24	11 36	
12 13	14 19	IC ☓
14 06	16 16	
18 27	20 30	
19 12	21 17	

Strasbourg

4 45	12 21	☒ München
13 52	21 42	☒ München
Ⓒ 20 10	4 56	☒ München ⌁ ⊸

Ⓒ Ⓢ: ⑥, ⑦

Venezia SL

0 55¹)	8 45	⊸
9 57	16 30	☓

¹) Ⓦ: dp/ab 1 42

These are the 1986 schedules for the Rhine KD boat rides and the Romantic Road bus tour—both free with your Eurailpass. The boat schedule is for peak season. Boats go all year but not as often as in the summer. The bus ride goes daily between Munich and Wiesbaden (Frankfurt) from mid-March through early November. The Wurzburg-Fussen trip goes daily from mid-May until early October each year.

Romantic Road Bus Tour

Europabus 190

V	W			W	X
....	....	0815	dep. *Frankfurt (Hbf.)* .... arr.	1955	....
0900	....	1015	dep. **Würzburg** (Hbf.) .... arr.	1809	....	1920
1005	....		dep. Bad Mergentheim .... dep.		....	1815
1200	....	1135	arr.⎫ Rothenburg/*Tauber* ⎰dep.	1700		1700
1330	....	1345	dep.⎭ ⎱arr.	1515		1535
1415	....	1430	dep. Feuchtwangen .... dep.	1430	....	1455
1430	....	1445	arr.⎫ Dinkelsbühl ⎰dep.	1415		1440
1500	....	1530	dep.⎭ ⎱arr.	1235		1310
1525	....	1605	dep. Nördlingen .... dep.	1155	....	1230
1610	....	1635	dep. Donauwörth .... dep.	1105	....	1200
1705	....	1735	arr.⎫ **Augsburg** (Hbf.) ⎰dep.	1020		1110
1715	....	1740	arr.⎭ ⎱arr.	1010		1100
1935	....		arr. **Füssen** (Postamt) .... dep.			0815
....	....	1855	arr. *München (Hbf.)* .... dep.	0900	....

Europabus 189

V					V	
....	0715	....	dep. Mannheim (Hbf.) .... arr.	....	2045	....
....	0745	....	dep. Heidelberg (Hbf.) .... arr.	....	2025	....
....	1200	....	arr. Rothenburg/Tauber .... dep.	....	1650	....

V— Daily, June 2–Sept. 28.   **W**—Daily, March 16–Nov. 4.   **X**— Daily, June 2–Sept. 29.

Rhine Cruise

SUMMER SERVICE ONLY: APRIL 4–OCTOBER 26 (NO SERVICE IN WINTER)
For the through services Rotterdam–Mannheim–Basel and v.v., see Table 350.

One class only.

m.v. Berlin. m.v. Bonn. m.v. Deutsches Eck.
m.v. Drachenfels. m.v. Düsseldorf. m.v. Frankfurt.
p.s. Goethe. m.v. Koblenz. m.v. Köln. m.v. Loreley.
p.s. Mainz. m.v. Rhein. m.v. Rheingold. p.s. Rüdesheim.
m.v. Stolzenfels. m.v. Trier. m.v. Wiesbaden.

A reduced service operates on July 6 and Aug. 10.

Tar. km		S	D	Exp O	N	U	X	E	H	P	C§	A	V	G	C	Q	F	H	J	M	B
100 Koblenz	arr.			1100				1120		1335	1356		1355			1545		1710		1900	
100 Koblenz	dep.	0900	1105			1130	1130	1340	1400	1400	1400	1400	1430	1430						1903	
105 Niederlahnstein	dep.	0924				1155	1155						1425	1455						1915	
112 Braubach	dep.	0958				1225	1225						1456	1525						1950	
121 Boppard	dep.	0900	1040	1130			1250	1315	1315	d	1525	1525			1545	1615					2030	
137 St. Goarshausen	dep.	1010	1150		1330	1330	1400	1430	1430			1625	1625			1655	1725				
137 St. Goar	dep.	1015	1155		1150	1340	1340	1405	1440	1440			1630	1630			1705	1735			
154 Bacharach	dep.	1120	1255		1120	1445	1445	1505	1545	1545			1725	1725			1810	1840			
166 Assmannshausen	dep.	1225	1350		1536	1540	1600	1640	1640			1810	1810			1905	1935			
170 Bingen	dep.	1255	1420		1228	1602	1610	1630	1710	1710			1835	1835			1930	2000			
172 Rüdesheim	dep.	1310	1430		1233	1620	1620	1640	1720	1720			1850	1850			1940	2010			
187 Eltville	arr.					1725	1745	1825	1825			1955	1955							
195 Wiesbaden-Biebrich	arr.	1300				1800	1810	1835	1910	1910			2040	2040							
200 Mainz	arr.	1310	1819	1830	1855	1930	1930			2100	2100									
225 Frankfurt/Main	arr.			2130s																	

Tar. km		R	L‡	L	X	J		F		B	N	U	Y	E	T	E		P	O	J	K
25 Frankfurt/Main	dep.							0715e													
0 Mainz	dep.	0845	0845								1015	1015		1045						1425	
5 Wiesbaden-Biebrich	dep.	0905	0905								1035	1035		1105						1433	
13 Eltville	dep.	0925	0925											1055		1125					
28 Rüdesheim	dep.	1025	1025	0950	0950						1145	1145		1220	1400	1400			1500	1550	1620	
30 Bingen	dep.	1045	1045	1010	1010									1235	1415	1415			1505	1605	1635	
34 Assmannshausen	dep.	1100	1100	1025	1025						1200	1200		1250	1430	1430				1615	1648	
46 Bacharach	dep.	1130	1130	1055	1055						1240	1240		1325	1505	1505				1730	1800	
63 St. Goar	dep.	1200	1200	1135	1135									1410	1550	1550				1730	1800	
63 St. Goarshausen	dep.	1210	1210	1145	1145						1315	1325		1420	1600	1600			1540	1740	1810	
72 Boppard	dep.	1250	1250	1235	1235									1510	1645	1645	d		1555	1820	1850	
80 Braubach	dep.	1315	1315	1305										1540	1715	1715				1850	1920	
95 Niederlahnstein	dep.		1330											1602	1737	1737				1912	1942	
100 Koblenz	arr.	1345	1345	1350										1620	1755	1755		1700	1618	1930	2000	
100 Koblenz	dep.		1405											1550	1625			1800	1705	1620		

A— Daily, Apr. 4–30.
B— Suns., May 5–June 9.
C— Daily, May 1–Sept. 16.
D— Daily, April 5–Oct. 27.
E— Daily, June 13–Sept. 16.
F— Daily, April 20–Sept. 16, also Apr. 6, 7, 13, 14.
G— Daily, Sept. 17–Oct. 27.
H— Daily, Sept. 17–Oct. 7.
J— Daily, Oct. 8–27.
K— Daily, April 5–Oct. 7.
L— Daily, May 1–Oct. 7.
M— Daily, June 16–Sept. 16 (not Andernach–Boppard on Sats.).
N— Daily, May 1–June 15; daily except Fris., June 16–Sept. 16.
O— Express service, daily except Mons., May 1–Oct. 20 by hydrofoil *Rheinpfeil*. Also runs Sats. and Suns., Apr. 6–28 and daily Oct. 25–27. Special fares apply.
P— Mons., June 17–Sept. 30, also Tues. and Thurs. July 2–Aug. 8.
Q— Sats. and Suns., June 29–Aug. 11.
R— Daily, Apr. 5–30 and Oct. 8–20 (also Rüdesheim–Koblenz, Oct. 21–28).
S— Daily, June 9–Sept. 16.
T— Daily, June 9–15.
U— Daily, Sept. 17–29.
V— Daily except Mons., Sept. 17–29.
W— Daily, May 12–Oct. 13.
X— Daily, Oct. 8–20.
Y— Daily except Mons., Sept. 17–29, also Sats. and Suns., June 29–Aug. 11.
c— Daily, May 18–June 15; daily except Fris., June 16–Sept. 16 (also May 4, 5, 11, 12).
d— Rhine/Moselle excursions to/from Kobern (Moselle).
e— 10 mins. later, Sept. 17–Oct. 7.
‡— Fast ship, supplement payable (not applicable between Koblenz and Köln Sept. 17–Oct. 7).
§— Fast ship supplement applicable only from Koblenz to Mainz.

BACK DOOR CATALOG

ALL ITEMS FIELD TESTED, HIGHLY RECOMMENDED,
COMPLETELY GUARANTEED AND DISCOUNTED BELOW RETAIL.

Combination Suitcase/Rucksack . . .$60.00

At 9″ x 21″ x 13″ this specially designed, sturdy, functional bag is maximum carry-on-the-plane size (fits under the seat). Made of rugged waterproof Cordura nylon, with hide-away shoulder straps, waist belt (for use as a rucksack), top and side handles, and a detachable shoulder strap (for toting as a suitcase). Perimeter zippers allow easy access to the room (2200 cu. in.) central compartment. Two small outside pockets are perfect for maps and other frequently used items. Over 6,000 Back Door travelers have used these bags around the world. Comparable bags cost much more. Available in navy blue, black, gray, or burgundy.

Moneybelt $6.00

Required! Ultra-light, sturdy, under-the-pants, nylon pouch just big enough to carry the essentials comfortably. I'll never travel without one and I hope you won't either. Beige, nylon zipper, one size fits all, with instructions.

Catalog . . . . .Free

For a complete listing of all the books, products, and services Rick Steves and Europe Through the Back Door offer you, ask us for a copy of our 32-page catalog. It's free.

Eurailpasses

With each Eurailpass order we offer a free taped trip consultation. Send a check for the cost of the pass you want along with your legal name, a proposed itinerary and a list of questions and we'll send you your pass, a taped evaluation of your plans, and all the train schedules and planning maps you'll need. Because of this unique service, we sell more train passes than anyone in the Pacific Northwest.

Back Door Tours

We encourage independent travel, but for those who want a tour in the Back Door style, we do offer a 22-day "Best of Europe" tour. For complete details, write to us at the address below.

All orders will be processed within one week and include a rubber universal sink stopper and one year's subscription to our Back Door Travel newsletter. Sorry, no credit cards. Send checks to:

Europe Through the Back Door
120 Fourth Ave. N.
Edmonds, WA 98020
tel. (206) 771-8303

Travel Guides from
John Muir Publications

I'd like to order the terrific travel guides checked below...

Quantity	Title	Each	Total
	Europe Through the Back Door—*Steves*	$11.95	
	Europe 101: History Art & Culture for Travelers—*Steves*	$9.95	
	Europe in 22 Days—*Steves*	$5.95	
	Mexico in 22 Days —*Rogers & Rosa*	$5.95	
	Spain & Portugal in 22 Days—*Steves*	$5.95	
	Complete Guide to Bed & Breakfasts, Inns & Guesthouses In the U.S. & Canada—*Lanier*	$12.95	
	Elegant Small Hotels—*Lanier*	$12.95	
	The People's Guide to Mexico (Revised)—*Franz*	$11.95	
	Asia Through the Back Door—*Steves & Gottberg*	$11.95	
		Subtotal	$
		Shipping	$1.75
		Total Enclosed	$

Non-U.S. payments must be in U.S. funds drawn on a U.S. bank.

METHOD OF PAYMENT (CHECK ONE)
☐ Charge to my (circle one):   MasterCard   VISA
☐ Check or Money Order Enclosed (Sorry, no CODs or Cash)
Credit Card Number

☐☐☐☐☐☐☐☐☐☐☐☐☐☐☐☐☐

Expiration Date ☐☐–☐☐

Signature x _____
　　　　　　Required for Credit Card Purchases
Telephone: Office (___) _____ Home (___) _____

Name _____

Address _____

City _____ State _____ Zip _____

Send to: John Muir Publications
P.O. Box 613
Santa Fe, NM 87504-0613
(505) 982-4078

Please allow 4-6 weeks for delivery.